Report of an Expedition
to
Copper, Tanana, and Koyukuk Rivers
In The
Territory of Alaska

A reprint of Allen's 1885 Journal

Foreword and Introduction by

Dwaine Schuldt

PO Box 221974 Anchorage, Alaska 99522-1974
books@publicationconsultants.com—www.publicationconsultants.com

ISBN 978-1-59433-109-1
Library of Congress Catalog Card Number: 2009932666

Manufactured in the United States of America.

Introduction

In the true story reflected in Lt. Allen's journal, you will learn of the generosity of Alaskan Natives. Lt. Allen's party would not have survived without adapting to the customs of the Alaskans and following their trails. They also would have starved without the food from the Alaskan people. This was the longest exploration of unknown land at this time in the world. Many quests had tried to go inland, but had not returned. This was mainly due to their ill treatment of the Natives. Lt. Allen traveled in a small party and welcomed the help of the Alaskans. He writes here in his journal from a traveler's perspective, not from the traditional military aspect. They traveled through the heart of this great land called Alyeska. The three great rivers they traveled had been explored very little by miners or trappers. This was a land largely unexplored by white people, but where Natives had already lived for more than 10,000 years. Lt. Allen's journal is published here from the original journal published in 1887. I would like to share this with you, who love to read of history and learn about Alaska. Enjoy the view of Alaska in the 1800s from Lt. Allen's journal descriptions of the land and the people.

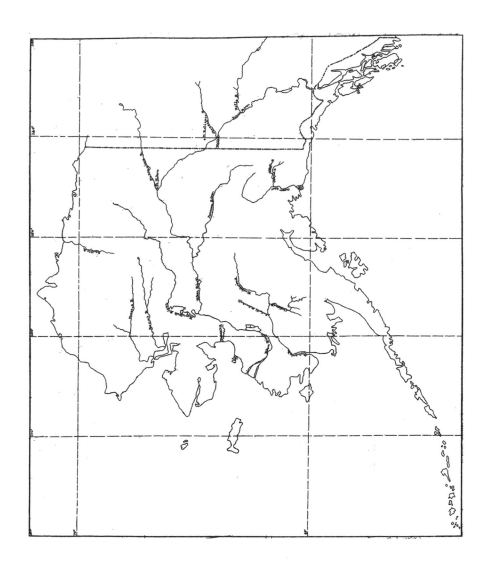

Foreword

I was fishing on the Copper River and thinking about how much this area of Alaska has not changed since the Allen expedition came through in 1885. The expedition's goal was to learn about Alaska for the government of the United States. The expedition was putting this unknown land on the map— they were creating the maps.

This story is from the heart of a man in the army, but writes from a perspective of a traveler in a strange land. The Allen expedition covered a vast land the size of the 1885 United States in a short time. They were short on food, no shelter for winter—but alive. The village near Chitina was also short on food, and the Natives still took the Allen party in. They all survived by sharing, hunting together, and being friends. This journal is a story of hardships and sharing. Neither group knew each other's language, and each were told stories of what to expect in an encounter. It is probably lucky, in their first meeting, that they were all starving. Their relationship that winter with the Chitina Athabascans is what helped them survive the rest of the expedition.

They knew to be cautious, but to be humble and strong. Moving everyday through unknown territory, they were pushed to extremes of Mother Nature at her best. They suffered the torment of bugs, freezing glacial waters, and lack of food. But everyone survived, and with such a small party of only three main expedition members, it has to be one of the smallest.

The adventure is still here in Alaska. I brought a friend to the river for the first time recently to dip net for fish. We jet-boated down into the canyon. I showed her how to hold her net, and boom—in less than 10 minutes she had a 50-pound king salmon. It was an adventure of exploration, but on a smaller scale than Allen's.

Read and enjoy this true adventure. Bring back to life one of my exploration heroes. What follows is Allen's journal as it was published in 1887. I wish I had been there!

Dwaine Schuldt
Anchorage, Alaska
Explorer of all 50 United States, Canada, Greenland, New Zealand, South America, and Antarctica.

REPORT

OF

AN EXPEDITION

TO

THE COPPER, TANANA, AND KÓYUKUK RIVERS,

IN THE

TERRITORY OF ALASKA,

IN

THE YEAR 1885,

"FOR THE PURPOSE OF OBTAINING ALL INFORMATION WHICH WILL
BE VALUABLE AND IMPORTANT, ESPECIALLY TO THE
MILITARY BRANCH OF THE GOVERNMENT."

MADE UNDER THE DIRECTION OF

General **NELSON A. MILES,** Commanding the Department of the Columbia,

BY

LIEUT. HENRY T. ALLEN,

Second United States Cavalry.

WASHINGTON:
GOVERNMENT PRINTING OFFICE,
1887.

CONTENTS.

CORRESPONDENCE AND INTRODUCTION.

PART I.—HISTORICAL.

PART II.—NARRATIVE.

Part III.—MAPS AND TABLES OF DISTANCES.

Part IV.—NATIVES,

Part V.—OBSERVATIONS

Part VI.—METEOROLOGICAL.

CORRESPONDENCE.

LETTER OF THE SECRETARY OF WAR.

WAR DEPARTMENT,
Washington City, May 6, 1886.

The Secretary of War has the honor to transmit to the United States Senate the official report of Lieut. Henry T. Allen, Second Cavalry, of his exploration of the Copper, Tananá, and Koyukuk Rivers of Alaska, in the year 1885, with accompanying maps, photographs, and drawings thereof, the same being transmitted in response to Senate resolution of the 16th ultimo, as follows:

Resolved, That the Secretary of War be, and he is hereby, directed to transmit to the Senate the official report of Lieut. Henry T. Allen, Second United States Cavalry, of his exploration of the Copper, Tanana, and Koyukuk Rivers of Alaska, in the year 1885, for reference to the Committee on Printing.

WM. C. ENDICOTT,
Secretary of War.
The President pro tempore of the United States Senate.

ORDERS.

[Special Orders No. 16.]

HEADQUARTERS DEPARTMENT OF THE COLUMBIA,
Vancouver Barracks, Wash. Ter., January 27, 1885.

By authority of the Lieutenant-General of the Army, conveyed in telegram from Division Headquarters, of the 24th instant, Second Lieut. Henry T. Allen, Second Cavalry, acting aide-de-camp, is authorized to make a reconnaissance in Alaska, proceeding up the Copper River and down the Tananá River Valley.

Letter of instruction will be furnished him for his information and guidance.

Lieutenant Allen will be accompanied and assisted by Sergeant Cady Robertson, Troop E, Second Cavalry, and Private Frederick W. Fickett, Signal Corps, ordered to report to him for this purpose.

Lieutenant Allen, with his party, will proceed by the February steamer to Sitka, Alaska, at which place he will engage passage by the schooner *Leo*, or other conveyance, to Nuchek, the nearest practical harbor to the mouth of Copper River.

Lieutenant Allen will avail himself of every possible opportunity to report his position and future movements.

The Quartermaster's Department will furnish the necessary transportation for Lieutenant Allen and party, and the Subsistence Department will furnish the necessary subsistence from stores on hand.

Lieutenant Allen is appointed acting assistant quartermaster, acting commissary of subsistence, and acting ordnance officer of the expedition.

Upon completion of the duty contemplated, Lieutenant Allen will return to these headquarters.

By command of Major-General Pope:

H. CLAY WOOD,
Assistant Adjutant-General.

Official:

H. CLAY WOOD,
Assistant Adjutant-General.

INSTRUCTIONS.

HEADQUARTERS DEPARTMENT OF THE COLUMBIA,
Vancouver Barracks, Wash. Ter., January 27, 1885.

SIR: On your return from your journey to Nuchek, near the mouth of Copper River, Alaska, last month you expressed a strong desire to attempt explorations in that territory, and, as you are aware, I telegraphed Brigadier-General Miles, absent in Washington City, of your anxiety and your proposed plan of action.

General Miles indicated his assent, and on his recommendation the Lieutenant-General commanding the Army, having read your report, has approved and authorized the proposed reconnaissance.

I inclose an official copy of Special Orders, No. 16, of this date, directing the movement of yourself and party, and communicate the following instructions, similar in import to those given Lieutenants Schwatka and Abercrombie, for your information and guidance.

In view of the fact that so little is known of the interior of the Territory of Alaska, and that the conflicting interests between the white people and the Indians of that Territory may in the near future result in serious disturbances between the two races, the department commander authorizes you to proceed to that Territory for the purpose of obtaining all information which will be valuable and important, especially to the military branch of the Government.

You will make your objective point that district of country drained by the Copper and Tananá Rivers, and ascertain as far as practicable the number, character, and disposition of all natives living in that section of country; how subdivided into tribes and bands; the district of country they inhabit; their relations to each other, and especially their disposition toward the Russian Government in the past, towards the United States Government in the past and at the present time, and toward the whites who are making their way into that region.

You will further examine their modes of life and their means of communication from one part of the country to the other, the amount and kinds of material of war in their possession and from whence obtained. You will further obtain such information as may be practicable as to the character of the country or means of using and sustaining a military force, if one should be needed in that territory. You will examine especially as to the kind and extent of the native grasses, and ascertain if animals ordinarily used in military operations can be subsisted and made of service there; also ascertain the character of the climate, especially inland, the severity of the winters, and any other information which would be important and valuable to the military service.

Let your researches be thorough, and endeavor to complete as far as practicable all desired information in each portion of the country as you advance into the interior, that your work may be resumed hereafter, if deemed necessary; at any point at which you may be compelled by untoward circumstances to abandon it.

You will endeavor to impress the natives with the friendly disposition of the Government, and in this connection the importance of opening and maintaining friendly relations with the natives cannot be too strongly impressed upon you and your assistants.

In no case will you move in any section of the country where you cannot go without provoking hostilities or inciting the natives to resistance.

You are not authorized to exercise any control of affairs in that Territory.

Whenever an opportunity occurs you will make full reports to these headquarters, accompanied as far as possible with itineraries, maps, tracings, and field notes of your journey and observations.

You will endeavor to reach the mouth of Copper River at least by the first of March, so as to ascend the river by the ice.

It is probable that the schooner *Leo* will, during February, make a trip from Sitka to Nuchek, and it is hoped you will be able to secure passage for your party by the *Leo*, and at the rate you have named—$70 each

If you are in all respects fortunate and successful, it is possible for you to ascend the Copper River and descend the Tananá, and return in 1885, and 'this will be your general instruction; but under the peculiar circumstances which will inevitably surround you, much must be left to your discretion and judgment, and therefore regarding your movements after leaving Copper River no definite directions can be given you.

You will at all times exercise careful and strict economy in your necessary expenditures.

You are authorized, in rejoining these headquarters, after completion of the duties assigned you, to arrange for the transportation of yourself and party to any point on the Pacific coast not south of San Francisco, from which you can communicate with these headquarters.

You will supply yourself with such necessary blanks pertaining to the Quartermaster's, Subsistence, and Ordnance Departments as may be requisite, and the necessary enlistment blanks, muster-out rolls, and discharges.

Should you find it necessary, you can enlist five Indian scouts.

Maj. De Witt C. Poole, paymaster, has been instructed to transfer to you $2,000, public funds of the Pay Department, as an advance to pay yourself and members of your detachment.

You know the conflicting dispatches which have been received in regard to this reconnaissance, and the difficulties the adjutant-general of the department has encountered.

All the hesitation in issuing the special order for the movement has arisen from the conflicting instructions received and a firm resolve not to see you leave on this distant and uncertain expedition without the most ample provision in supplies and public funds to insure your safety, comfort, and the success of the reconnaissance.

You now have ample funds; they are to be used for the payment of yourself and party; but so long as you have them you will not suffer from hunger or permit your party to.

With best wishes for your success and safe return.

By command of Major-General Pope:

H. CLAY WOOD,
Assistant Adjutant-General.

Second Lieut. HENRY T. ALLEN,
Second Cavalry, Acting Aide-de-Camp,
Commanding Expedition to Alaska.

LETTER OF TRANSMITTAL.

WAR DEPARTMENT, ADJUTANT-GENERAL'S OFFICE,
Washington, April 9, 1886.

SIR: I have the honor to transmit herewith, as per orders, the accompanying report of a reconnaissance on the Copper, Tananá, and Koyukuk Rivers of Alaska, made in the year 1885, together with maps illustrative of the country drained by said rivers, as far as the work extended.

Rivers and other geographical features actually seen are drawn in full. Previously unmapped information from other sources is indicated by dotted lines.

The reduction of sextant observations, which depended on a best-grade Howard movement watch, is not as satisfactory as I had hoped to obtain. Having had the benefit of a trip to Alaska before starting on this reconnaissance, I became convinced of the impracticability of carrying a box chronometer, nor have I since had reason to think that it could have withstood the hardships. Had it been carried on the person of any of the party it would have had many submersions in the rivers and jars from unexpected tumbles.

The services rendered by my assistants, Sergeant Cady Robertson, Troop E, Second Cavalry, and Private Fred. W. Fickett, United States Signal Corps, throughout the privations and hardships necessary to the success of the expedition, were most valuable, as will be seen from the report and records.

The prospectors, Peter Johnson and John Bremner, whom I added to the party, the former at Nuchek, the latter at the junction of Copper and Chittyná Rivers, rendered most excellent services. I cannot say too much in commendation of the indomitable courage and energy of Mr. Johnson. His zeal and endurance were admirable.

I am under obligations to staff officers of the Department of Columbia, who so efficiently supplied the party from their respective departments with such necessaries as the conflicting circumstances under which we started would permit. Special acknowledgment is due to Col. H. Clay Wood, adjutant-general of the Department of the Columbia, for his conscientious fostering of the expedition. Acknowledgment is also due to Lieut. Commander H. E. Nichols, commanding *Pinta*, and officers of that vessel, for courtesies extended the party during the stay in Sitka and during the voyage to Nuchek; to Mr. Lewis Gerstle, president Alaska Commercial Company, for the privilege granted me in his letter of introduction to the various factors of that company in the Territory, authorizing them to cash checks and render such other assistance as was in their power; and to these gentlemen at Nuchek, on the Yukon, at St. Michael's, at the Seal Islands, and at Ounalaska.

The photography of Copper River, other than that obtained from Lieutenant Abercrombie, expresses in a poor manner the result of much patience and perseverance under the most trying circumstances. The plates were necessarily intrusted to natives to be carried to the mouth of the river. Recent developments show that their curiosity led them to open the box containing them, thus exposing the plates to the light, and totally injuring all but the few we had developed.

Attempt has been made in the detailed report to account for the incompleteness, in many respects, of the information obtained, but the difficulty of obtaining subsistence and transportation, and other unusual disadvantages, will partially account for the many omissions. Delays were impossible on account of scarcity of food and unwillingness to rest while ignorant of time required to overcome the obstacles in advance.

The loss of the psychrometer by theft of the natives on upper waters of the Tananá, and the injury they inflicted on the aneroid barometer, account for the absence of records from these instruments after the middle of June.

The U. S. revenue steamer *Corwin*, after her deeds of daring in the Arctic, anchored off Fort St. Michael's, and gallantly extended us passage to San Francisco, notwithstanding she was crowded with the unfortunate crews of wrecked whalers. I would express my sense of the many kindnesses and courtesies rendered the party by Capt. M. A. Healy, commanding, and all the officers of the *Corwin*. The great inconveniences these worthy gentlemen submitted to in order to afford us a return demand more than ordinary thanks.

When the party started it was not considered possible to do more than ascend the Copper River, cross the Alaskan Mountains, and descend the Tananá River in one season; yet verbal authority was obtained to continue the work, in case there was time, or, if it became necessary, to winter in the Territory; and this is the authority for the exploration of the Koyukuk River.

It is believed that the maps and information embodied in this report will be valuable to prospectors and others who are now making their way into the interior of the country, to the geographical world, and to all who are interested in this possession of the United States, about which so little authentic information relative to its interior is known.

Very respectfully, your obedient servant,

H. T. ALLEN,
Second Lieutenant, Second Cavalry.

To the ADJUTANT-GENERAL,
United States Army.

INTRODUCTION

So much has been written with respect to the Alaskan country in general, its coast resources, peoples and their customs, that the following report will be restricted almost entirely to the interior, and especially to the vast extent of country drained by the Copper, Tananá, and Koyukuk Rivers, nearly all of which is unknown.

To those unacquainted with the extent of our Alaskan possessions, the distances recorded during the explorations would seem exaggerated. Observation of the accompanying map showing the number of degrees of latitude and longitude covered by the exploration, and a recollection that the area of Alaska is equal to three times that of New England, New York, Pennsylvania, New Jersey, and Maryland taken together, will suffice to account for the seemingly excessive distances.

The work is included between the sixtieth and sixty-seventh parallels, and between the one hundred and forty-secondth and one hundred and sixty-first meridians, and these inclose approximately 240,000 square miles.

It is a very remarkable fact that a region under a civilized government for more than a century should remain so completely unknown as the vast territory drained by the Copper, Tananá, and Koyukuk Rivers,

15

PART I.

HISTORICAL

HISTORICAL.

COPPER RIVER.

The knowledge of Copper or Atná River prior to 1884 was limited to Russian records and native reports.

The initial point for all expeditions to that river has been Port Eteches (Nuchek) or Hinchinbrook Island, now the trading station of the Alaska Commercial Company, and about 50 miles to the westward of the mouth of Copper River.

This village was located by Cook in 1776-'79; by Chornhoff in 1830; Belcher in 1836-'42; Tebénkoff in 1852; and, more recently, by the Coast and Geodetic Survey, which last gives it a latitude of 60° 21′ N. and longitude of 146° 38′ W.

From 1788, the year when the first redoubt (odinátschka) was built at the mouth of the river, up to 1847, the explorations were made by men wholly destitute of mathematical knowledge, and the maps constructed by them were subsequently found to be entirely inaccurate.

The odinátschka ("a single redoubt") was located a few miles south of Alagánik (Anahánuk), but at present no traces of it remain. It is probable that a village of two miserable barábarras, called by the natives "Skátalis," is on the site of the old odinátischka of the Russians.

The mouth of Copper River was discovered by Nagaieff in 1781.

In 1796 there were two expeditions having for their object the exploration of Copper River, one under Tarchánoff, the other under Samóyleff, both of which failed, the latter on account of hostility of the natives.

In 1798 Partíchken, and in 1803 Bóyanoff, explored the Copper River for a short distance. In 1819 Klimóosky made some explorations in the same direction. In 1843 Gregórieff (Grijorjew of the Germans) renewed the attempt.

In 1847 Captain Tebénkoff directed Rufus Seréberinikoff, a creole,* and a graduate of a school of commercial navigation of Saint Petersburg, to explore the Copper River.

---

*The term Creole, misapplied to mixed races of the Russian-American possessions, formerly signified the offspring of a Russian father and native mother. At the present time there are many so-called Creoles in Alaska, some of whom have a Russian grandfather and an American father. In many the native blood predominates. A former master of the schooner Leo, who had married a Creole of the Aleutian Islands, informed me that there were at that time (1884) only two "pure blood" Russian women in Alaska.

The unfortunate Seréberinikoff, with his assistants, eleven in number, a part at least of whom were Aleuts, were murdered somewhere north of the Tleschitina, a river known at the present time by the natives as Tezliná, and such I have called it in my report. No cause or place of his death has ever been definitely assigned, and the meager results of his explorations are known from his partially destroyed notes, subsequently given up by the natives. It is true that one of his observations for latitude gave 62° 48′ N., but there is no record of his journey after he had descended the Tezliná and started again up the Copper. The mouth of the Tezliná is in approximate latitude 62° N.

On the 14th of August, 1847, Seréberinikoff arrived at Alagánik, on the most westerly channel of the delta of the Copper River, called by him Anee River. His observation placed this village in latitude 60° 41′ 17″, while the records show it to be only a few miles above the *odinátschka*. Lieutenant Abercrombie places it in latitude 60° 21′, and the latter has been used by me. Continuously cloudy and stormy weather prevented an observation in this locality during our travels.

The following is the gist of Seréberinikoff's notes. The Russian party left Alagánik, intending to row up the river, but meeting a current of nine miles per hour, was compelled to cordell.

On the 18th the northernmost end of this channel (the Anee) was reached, some floating ice having been encountered *en route*. At the upper end of the channel were numerous shallows.

On August 26, eight days after reaching the main stream, the latitude was determined to be 60° 38′ 47″. I will here remark that this observation is probably the authority for the very singular position of the mouth of Copper River, as shown on all existing charts prior to that of Lieutenant Abercrombie. It is evident that either the observation is much out, or else the delta mouth of the river has undergone a wonderful change since 1848. I found the course of the river from Alagánik, by following the western channels as much as possible, to be nearly north. I do not doubt that radical changes are being wrought in the delta of the river by the enormous deposits annually carried down, but the one in question seems too great to have been accomplished in a period of thirty-seven years.

On September 1 Seréberinikoff's boat struck a hidden rock, and many valuable articles, including his watch, were lost.

September 4, his party reached the *odinátschka*, below the mouth of the Tschichitna (Chittyná), where it wintered. The coldest weather recorded was 40 below zero (Reamur).

May 16, 1848, Seréberinikoff started for the upper river with eleven men, one hundred fish, four poods (thirty-six pounds each) of biscuits, four wild sheep, and some tea and sugar.

At noon on the 17th the party passed the mouth of the Chittyná. On the 18th stopped at a settlement of twelve souls, where the inhabitants were suffering fearfully from destitution and hunger, and on the following day it arrived at a settlement of twelve souls, six women and six children, the five men usually dwelling there having gone to Constantine Redoubt (Nuchek). Here the party was treated to fish-bones, and some roots, and in return gave two pounds of tobacco.

On the 20th it reached a deserted settlement, whose inhabitants had left in March for a hunt.

On the 22d the sheep were all gone and the men put on one fish per day.

On the 24th reached mouth of Tezliná, flowing from Lake Plavéznie. Men put on one-half fish per day. The Tezliná was found to be shallow, full of stones, and very rapid.

On the 25th started on foot to explore Lake Plevéznie, keeping the Tezliná in sight.

On the 28th made a halt on a small river and met two families of natives returning from a hunt. Were treated to fresh moose meat, and gave them in turn two pounds of tobacco. Observation for latitude gave 62° 8′ 11″.

On the 30th reached the lake; found two families. At night the natives killed four deer (*caribou?*), swimming in the lake. Purchased one for 135 feet of beads. All of it was at once eaten, together with some dry meat and some small fish. Red fish (salmon, doubtless) appear in the middle of June. It is said they never go down the river again. Natives of Plavéznie have the same language, same destitution and constant suffering as do those of Copper River. Hunger begins the middle of winter, however abundant the game of the preceding season. The greatest reliance for food is on rabbits, which they snare.

June 3, built a *baidárra* and passed two days in following around the shores of the lake. The southeastern end of it is near a chain of mountains capped with ice, below the line, of which timber grows. From the west side the lake receives two tributaries, along one of which is the portage to the Bay of Kenái, to make which requires about twelve days. Trees on southern shores only. Latitude of southerly point of lake is 62° 2′ 32″. Poverty of natives leads to the conclusion that there would be little fur trade.

June 5, took leave of the friendly natives and started down the Tezliná in a baidárra; reaching its mouth the following day. Thence up the Copper River. From this time there are no records, save the observation, which gives a latitude of 62° 48′ 45″.

I have had the above translated from the "Journal of the Russian Geographical Society," published at St. Petersburg in 1849, now in the Congressional Library, by Mr. S. N. Buynitzi, and have gone thus into detail to show that the nomadic habits of the natives, their improvidence, and the annual scarcity of food during the winter months existed forty years ago as well as to-day. The above narrative, so far as I know, is all that is of record relative to the Tezliná River and Lake Plevéznie. It partially accounts for the origin of the Midnoóskies' present insatiate desire for tobacco. The watch having been lost early in September, 1847, there were no determinations of longitude.

From Nicolai, one of the most intelligent of the Midnoóskies (the name given to the Copper River natives by the Russians), I learned that there had been three massacres of Russians on the Copper River, one above Tarál and two below. The one above, probably that of Seréberinikoff, he claims was done by the Tatlatáns, or Upper Copper River natives, the one near the mouth of the river by coast natives, and the one just below Tarál by his own people.

He was reluctant to talk about the matter, but finally vindicated his people by telling the wrongs inflicted on them by the Russians. His story was as follows: Three Russians and as many sleds drawn by natives were *en route* to Tarál with merchandise. The natives were not allowed to sleep, and were compelled to haul the Russians, who slept on the sleds. At a preconcerted sign the head of each of them was crushed in with an ax. He said he knew nothing about the details of the other massacres, and if he did he would not talk about them.

The following is from the Alaska Coast Pilot, part 1, published in 1869:

There is an Indian settlement at the mouth of the Tschettschitna [Chittyná], and when the ice breaks up in the lake the stream suddenly overflows its banks and rushes with such swiftness that the inhabitants flee to the mountains.

On the left bank of the Atna, a mile above the Tschettschitna, is the single house of one of the Russian company's traders. Tebénkoff places it in latitude 61° 28′ 01″ and longitude 145° 16′. On the left bank, directly in view of the post, is the sugar-loaf-shaped volcano, Mount Wrangell, covered with perpetual snow, but emitting fire and smoke. The natives of the river are described by Tebénkoff as savage, bloodthirsty, suspicious, stubborn, and unwilling to have anything to do with the Russians.

I saw no traces of this Indian settlement at the mouth of Tschettschitna (Chittyná), and if such existed it would probably have been situated on its banks, which are many feet higher than the line the water attained in the spring of 1885. Moreover, there is no lake of any considerable size at the head of the river, *if the natives can* in any manner be relied on. The only traces of a Russian store that I could ascertain to have ever existed are at the present village of Tarál, 2½ miles below the mouth of the Chittyná. I found Mount Wrangell to be on the east side of Copper River and 40 miles distant from the nearest point. Tebénkoff's information was derived from the data of Seréberinikoff, whom he sent out. I cite the above few extracts to show how the existing knowledge of the Copper River region differs from the country as we saw it.

The natives informed me that no white men had ever ascended the Chittyná River, and this is partially corroborated by the fact that in 1867 the officers of the Russian American Company supposed that pure copper was found in masses twenty-five or thirty miles above the mouth of the river.

In 1882 Mr. C. G. Holt, the present trader at Nuchek, ascended the Copper River with the Midnoóskies as far as Tarál, on their return to their own country, in the spring, and remained with them until September. He, however, returned to Nuchek without having been more than a mile or two from Tarál. His objective point was the copper region of the Chittyná; but having been crippled through some accident, his purpose was defeated. He described the natives as treacherous and thievish, detailing at the same time some incidents from which he drew his estimate of their character, and illustrated the imminent dangers to which they had exposed him.*

In the summer of 1884, Lieut. W. R. Abercrombie, Second Infantry, A. D. C., assisted by Captain Robinson, assistant surgeon, Lieutenant Brumback, Second Infantry, and C. A. Homan, assistant topographer, started up the Copper River with instructions from General N. A. Miles, commanding department, similar to those hereto prefixed. This party reached a position on the Copper River in latitude 60° 41', when it returned to Nuchek, and subsequently made explorations in the direction of Port Valdes.

The following is from the report of Lieutenant Abercrombie:

On the first day of September, being convinced of the unwarrantable risk of leaving our canoe and starting out on foot at the then late season without rations (ours being more or less damaged by having been so often immersed in the river), I felt satisfied that the only course left was a winter journey. Furthermore, we had been informed by the Upper River natives and those on the coast that a shorter route existed via Port Valdes over the mountain to a lake, the outlet of which ran into the Copper River below the Chechitna (Chittyná).

A full report of the operations of Lieutenant Abercrombie's party is in the possession of the War Department.

The miner, John Bremner, ascended the Copper as far as Tarál in the summer of 1884, and his subsequent actions are included in my report.

So far as I know the foregoing constituted our knowledge of the Copper River and its shed prior to 1885.

---

* About one year after our visit to Nuchek Mr. Holt was murdered by the Copper River natives, who seemed to cherish a violent dislike towards him during our intercourse with them.

TANANÁ RIVER.

The history of "white man's" exploits on the Tananá is indeed limited, and by omitting one or two events might be told in the history of the little trading station on the right bank 48 miles from the mouth of the river.

From "A Reconnaissance of the Yukon River," 1869, by Raymond, the following is taken:

Leaving Nulato on the 19th, we arrived at Fort Adams on the 22d. This station is near the mouth of the Tananá River, the most important tributary of the Yukon, and was at the time the easternmost station ever established on the river from the western coast. * * * Chief, indeed, among all the tributaries of the Yukon stands the great Tananá, "the river of the mountains." It empties into the Yukon about 30 miles below the Ramparts, and its rapid waters increase the current of the main river for a long distance. Only a few miles from the mouth have been traveled by white men. It apparently comes from the southeast, but it is believed that many miles above the explored portion it makes a great bend from the east, its sources lying near the Upper Yukon.

The following account is from "Alaska and its Resources," 1870, by Dall:

The Tananá River enters the Yukon in latitude 64° 07′ N. and in longitude 150° 08′ W., and is entirely unexplored. No white man has dipped his paddle into its waters and we only know of its length and character from Indian reports. They inform us that it flows from the eastward, that some of its headwaters are not far from Fort Yukon, and others not far distant from the Upper Ramparts of the Yukon, above the fort. The largest trees brought down in the spring freshets come from this river. Its banks are said to be high and mountainous and its course marked by rapids and cascades. The length is estimated at 250 miles. The name Tananá means River of Mountains, and it has long been described on the old maps of Russian America under the name of the River of the Mountain Men. The Hudson Bay men called it the Gens des Buttes River.

For a while after the transfer of the territory there were two rival companies in the Yukon country, each eager to obtain the furs of the natives of the Tananá, and this led to the establishment of a post on the north bank of the Tananá, 48 miles above its mouth.

This is the station where Mrs. Bean, the wife of the trader, was murdered in cold blood. Her slayer is yet at large, and the indifference to his crime manifested by our Government now causes the natives to make threats to the white traders, at the same time boasting of the immunity accorded Mrs. Bean's murderer. They also cite the massacre of Lieutenant Barnard and the Russian Kogénikoff, for which they have never been punished.

In the year 1882, the missionary, Mr. Simms, started with a few natives up the Tananá in canoes. The distance he ascended is not known, though it is supposed that the Toclat River was the limit of his travel. His food supplies became short, and the Yukon natives, through fear of the Tananatánas, refused to go farther, hence his return.

I met while in the territory several miners who had either started across from Fort Reliance for the Tananá or were going to start very soon. Up to the time I left that river none had ever reached its waters. The frequent visits of the Upper Tananatánas to the posts Fetútlin and Fort Reliance, on the Yukon, called by them *Tetatling* and *Sawchek*, respectively, have awakened in many of the miners who annually cross from Chilcat to the Yukon a strong desire to visit the country of these people. It is not the difficulties of the trail so much as its length that has thus far deterred them. To carry supplies on the back for that distance, and at the same time prospect, is a difficult task even for miners, the most hardy and capable class of men for such work.

Lieutenant Schwatka, in his official report of his reconnaissance on the Yukon in 1883, makes mention of the Tananá as the largest unexplored river of the western continent. In his "Along Alaska's Great River," published in 1885, an account of the journey from Fetútlin, near Johnny's Village, on the Yukon, to the Tananá, thence to its mouth, by Messrs. Harper and Bates, is given as follows :

With one white companion, and some Indians as packers, he crossed from the trading station at Belle Isle, near Johnny's Village, or Klatol-klin, in a southwest direction, over the hills that divide the Yukon and Tananá basins, ascending a tributary of the former and descending one of the latter, the journey occupying two or three weeks, after which the Indians were sent back. A boat was constructed from the hide of a moose, resembling the "bull boat" of the Western frontiersman, and in this they drifted to the river's mouth. At the point the two travelers first sighted the Tananá the trader estimated it to be about 1,200 yards wide, or very nearly three-quarters of a mile, and as they were floating fifteen or sixteen hours a day for ten days, on a current whose speed he estimated at 6 or 7 miles an hour, it being much swifter than the Yukon at any point as high as Belle Isle, my informant computed his progress at from 90 to 100 miles a day, or from 900 to 1,000 miles along the Tananá. He estimates the whole length of the river, by combining the result of his observation with Indian reports, at from ten to twelve hundred miles. Fear of the Tananá Indians appears to be the motive for the rapid rate of travel through their country and although in general a very friendly tribe to encounter away from home, they are always opposed to any exploration of their country. The trader's companion had suggested and promoted the journey as a quasi scientific expedition, and he collected a few skulls of the natives and some botanical specimens, but no maps or notes were made of the trip, and it was afterward said by the Alaska Company's employés that the explorer was an envoy of the "opposition,' as the old traders called the new company, sent to obtain information regarding the country as a trading district. Allowing a fair margin for all possible error, I think the river is from 800 to 900 miles long, not a single portion of which can be said to have been mapped. This would probably make the Tananá, if I am right in my estimate, the largest wholly unexplored river in the world, certainly the longest of the western continent.

Lieutenant Schwatka adds as a foot-note :

I have since learned that Mr. Bates made a map and took notes.

I traveled several days on the Yukon River with Mr. Harper and learned of him that his party had no instruments for determining positions while running down the Tananá. From his description of that part of the river first seen by it, and being informed by him that it was below the Bushy-haired chief's (Kheeltat's), I am disposed to think that it was just below Cathedral Rapids, about 100 miles from the mouth of the Tetling River. Mr. Harper considered his natives skilled men for running rapids and expressed great surprise that we had safely run the rapids of the Tananá without native assistance. He considered the chances of a party successfully running the rapids of the Tananá in a skin boat about equal to those in floating down the Yukon on a raft with natives on each bank firing at it.

These few paragraphs constitute the history of the third or fourth river in size in Alaska. I am in doubt whether this or the Koyukuk contains the greater volume of water.

KOYUKUK RIVER.

In the early part of the year 1833 the island of St. Michael's became known to Cook, and was called by him Cape Stephens. In the latter part of the same year Baron Wrangell, general manager of the Russian American colonies, with the idea that communication between Behring Sea and Norton Sound could be established overland, sent Tebénkoff to the latter place. While there Tebénkoff founded a settlement on "Cape Stephens," and called it and the island St. Michael's, the name now used. From this point the subsequent Russian exploring expeditions into the Yukon country toward the Yukon River started.

A Creole, Andrea Glásanoff, with four volunteers, was the first to make the portage from Norton Sound to the Yukon River, thence to the Kuskokwim, but his explorations did not extend farther up the Yukon than Anvik River.

In 1833 Lieutenant Rosenberg, I. R. N., was sent with a schooner to explore the mouths of the Yukon, called at the time the Kwikpak, but failed to do so on account of the shallow water there.

Five years later Málakoff, starting from St. Michael's in the interest of the Russian American Company, crossed from Kekigtowruk village to the Yukon and ascended it as far as the present site of Nuláto, 24 miles below the mouth of the Koyukuk River, where he established a trading station. For want of provisions he was compelled to return temporarily to St. Michael's, and while absent the natives burned the building he had constructed.

Besides these, Captain Kúprianoff, I. R. N., sent several expeditions prior to 1841 towards the Yukon, the main object of all being of commercial interest.

In 1841 Captain Etolin was directed to select a competent man for astronomical determination of places in the direction of Kótzebue Sound and in the interior. Lieutenant Zagóskin having been chosen for this work, arrived at St. Michael's July 10, 1842, with six volunteers from Sitka. August 1 he started up the coast to the mouth of the Únalaklík River, where he established a post of four men. Its object was to prevent the natives carrying their furs to those farther north, who traded them to the inhabitants (Chukchi) of the Asiatic side, and also to secure communication with the settlement which Málakoff had begun at Nuláto. For reasons best known to himself, Zagóskin determined not to attempt the summer portage, but wait until winter; hence his return to St. Michael's in the mean time.

On the 4th day of December, with five sleds and twenty-seven dogs, he again started for Únalaklík, which he reached in time to start for the Yukon on the 16th. Heavy snows caused the failure of this attempt, but another on the 30th was successful, and on January 10, 1843, he was at a settlement on the Yukon (Hogotlinda), lat. 64° 19'. Five days later he was at Nuláto, where he remained until February 25, when, in accordance with his instructions, he left the place to explore in the direction of Kótzebue Sound. To accomplish this he began the ascent of the Kóyukuk River (Yunáka). At its junction with the Yukon he found a settlement of considerable size, called by the natives Tokákat.

March 4 he was at the junction of the Koteelkákat with the Koyukuk (56 miles by the river from the Yukon and his highest point on the Koyukuk). From this point he endeavored to reach an arm of Kótzebue Sound by following up the Koteelkákat, probably 30 or 40 miles, thence across the country to his destination. The natives he had employed, after having gone a great part of the distance, refused to advance farther through fear of the Máhlemutes, so Zagóskin was compelled to return via the Kóyukuk without having accomplished all his mission. The highest point reached by him in the direction of the Koteelkákat is in latitude 65° 35', about 20 miles north of its mouth.

The above is the gist of an abstract from Lieutenant Zagóskin's journal, by S. I. Zelónai, a member of St. Petersburg Geographical Society, afterwards minister of roads for Russia.

The following account of his explorations is given in the History of Alaska, by H. H. Bancroft, 1885:

In 1842, Lieutenant Zagóskin, of the imperial navy, set forth for Norton Sound and Mikhillovsk (St. Michael's), purposing to make an inland exploration of the northern territory. His work was confined chiefly to the middle course of the Kuskokwim and the lower course of the Yukon, especially the Kóyukuk, which he followed to its headwaters, and to the divide which separates it from the streams running into Kotzebue Sound. At Nuláto he was assisted by Derzhabin (Derabin?) in building a new fort. Zagóskin's exploration was performed conscientiously and well. Whenever we find mistakes we may ascribe them to his imperfect instruments and to local obstacles.

That Zagóskin went to the headwaters of the Koteelkákat I do not doubt, but I have failed to find any authority for the statement that he reached those of the Kóyukuk.

Dall is the authority for the following, which is additional proof of the want of accurate knowledge of the size of the Kóyukuk:

The Kóyukuk River enters from the north, and is a large stream, formed by the fusion of the Kuthlatino and Kutelno Rivers from the west, and the Koteelkákat from the east. Its length, including tributaries, is estimated at 100 miles. Other rivers, rising near it, fall into Kotzebue and Norton Sounds.

He too was probably, at the time of writing, under the impression that Zagóskin had reached its headwaters.

The officers and employés of the Western Union Telegraph expedition made many explorations in Western Alaska shortly after the transfer of the Territory in 1868 (see Dall's works). Some of the American fur traders established a post at the junction of the Koteelkákat and Kóyukuk to intercept the furs that would be delivered at Nuláto. The competition that existed between rival trading companies caused the fur trade to become so unremunerative that finally the Alaska Commercial Company was left alone in charge of the business. The rivalry no longer existing. the post on the Kóyukuk was abandoned and has so remained since.

The engineer of the steamboat *Yukon*, a Canadian, informed me that he had been to the Kóyukuk in winter via the trail from Nuklúkyet. I afterwards learned that not only he but Mr. Mayo, a fur trader, had been to the small village on the Konoótena, a tributary of the Kóyukuk, but no farther. It is hardly probable that any white man had, prior to our journey, seen that portion of the Kóyukuk above the abandoned trading station.

Captain Raymond, as early as 1869, heard of the trail from near Nuklúkyet (Fort Adams) to the Kóyukuk. He describes from native reports as follows:

From the headwaters of the Koteelkákat River, the eastern branch of the Koyukuk River, which empties into the Yukon a few miles above Nuláto, the natives are said to make a portage to the headwaters of the Quisnon, and descending this and the Tosecárgut River, of which it is a western tributary, to make their way to Fort Adams. I have no information regarding the character of the country in the vicinity of these streams.

On the 13th we passed the mouth of the Kóyukuk, the largest northern tributary of the Yukon River, I believe, although little or nothing is known any great distance beyond its mouth.

The "historical" of this river, so far as relates to the exploits of white men, is easily and quickly summed up. The *study of the* history of the natives, however, is highly interesting, but not by any means so determinate a one.

PART II.

NARRATIVE.

THE VOYAGE AND ARRIVAL.

PORTLAND, OREGON, TO NUCHEK, ALASKA.

The time of starting of the party was not definitely determined until a few hours prior to the departure of the mail-steamer *Idaho*. She was boarded at Portland, Oregon, at 11 p. m., January 28, and departed for Puget Sound at daylight the following day. The first port touched was Townsend at midnight, January 29. From this point the usual route was followed to Sitka, touching at the following places: Victoria and Nanaimo, on Vancouver's Island, British Columbia; Wrangell, Juneau, and a few other places of less importance.

A few purchases of quartermaster and subsistence stores were made at Townsend and Victoria, also some sleds at Juneau, such as are used by the miners of the Stickeen River country. These sleds are described further on.

We reached Sitka February 10, and found, much to my chagrin, that the schooner *Leo*, on which the transportation of party to Nuchek was contemplated, had sailed two days prior to San Francisco. That this disappointment was not the result of a breach of promise on the part of her owners did not mitigate in any degree our difficulties. Transportation on her was conditionally agreed upon between Mr. Whitford, of Sitka, and myself, a few months prior, with the understanding that I notify him by January steamer whether or not it would be wanted. At the very last moment I telegraphed to Nanaimo, British Columbia, the limit of telegraphic communication in the direction of Alaska: "There will be no Government party on February steamer"; and this released the schooner, since she failed to receive letters and telegrams addressed to her at San Francisco, where it is supposed she would be during December and part of January, instead of in Puget Sound, where I afterwards found she had staid during this time. The telegram was carried from Nanaimo to Sitka by the January steamer, and expressed at the time the supposed intentions of the Government. The steamer that left Portland, Oreg., the last of December is called the January steamer, inasmuch as most of January is consumed in making both ways. At Townsend, on January 30, I learned that the *Leo* had cleared for Sitka, and this caused me to suppose that our arrival would find her there.

There is nothing not frequently previously described by others to be related of the passage of the mail steamer to Sitka.

The immediate point of departure for the interior of Alaska was Núchek, on Hinchinbrook Island, 432 miles distant by sea from Sitka and 50 miles from mouth of Copper River. It here seemed impossible to engage available transportation to either point. The *Idaho* would not consent to go, on account of it being the season of storms, and the want of a sufficient supply of coal aboard. Lieutenant-Commander Nichols, U. S. Navy, would not move the *Pinta* without orders from the Navy Department. The Thlinkit Indians would not attempt the voyage at that season of the year in their canoes, though a few annually visit the Yakutat natives for trading purposes. These latter trade at Nuchek, and through them transportation there was contemplated. An effort was finally made to secure a crew of white men, half-breeds, and natives with which to man on old row and sail boat of a peculiar type found at Sitka, and in this it was intended to follow the coast around to Nuchek. The money offered these men was a great inducement, and all agreed at first, but finally refused, giving as their reason the danger of such an attempt. As a last resort I went to Kilisnoo on the *Idaho*, with a view of chartering the small steamboat used by the Northwest Fur and Trading Company at its fishery, but in this endeavor the same obstacles were met.

My efforts, together with other feasible methods, were recorded and sent on steamer *Idaho* to headquarters Department of the Columbia for consideration.

From Kilisnoo I returned to Sitka (70 miles) by canoe, and remained until the return of the *Idaho*, March 11, 1885. In the mean time I continued to make preparations for the interior by overhauling and repacking the supplies, of which there were about one thousand rations. At the same time we were familiarizing ourselves with our instruments, which were the sextant and artificial horizon, a best grade watch of Howard movement, used as chronometer, camera with dry plates and chemicals, and barometer. Besides these we had a pocket sextant, aneroid barometer, psychrometer, prismatic and pocket compasses. I found the pocket sextant to be unsatisfactory. The position of index arm, when it was supposed to be fixed, was unstable on account of the loose fittings of the gearings on which it depended. During this unexpected delay we added many articles that insufficient time below had prevented our collecting to our small outfit, yet was I by no means sanguine that all we already had could be carried. Among the valuable articles added were Liebig's extract of beef, other sleds, and sleeping bags of linen sail cloth, made thoroughly waterproof by the use of beeswax and linseed oil. To Lieut. T. Dix Bolles, executive officer of the *Pinta*, we were indebted for them.

The *Idaho*, on her arrival at Sitka, March 11, brought the authority given Lieutenant-Commander Nichols to convey my party to Núchek, a copy of which I received. This long delay had, I was well aware, imperiled our prospects of ascending the Copper River on the ice. The *Pinta* loosed her moorings on the morning of the 13th, and left the dock on the 16th, bound for Núchek. This voyage was without special note, save the fogs we encountered near Middleton Island, which caused some delay.

On the afternoon of the 19th the *Pinta* steamed into Núchek Harbor, to remain only a few hours. Our outfit, including provisions, having been carefully packed and reduced as much as possible in volume, was soon landed in the row-boats, the anchorage having been made off Phipp's Point, about one mile from the landing.

The Department is already in possession of descriptions of the Indian village Núchek, the natives, trading stores, and surroundings, from the report recently submitted by Lieut. W. R. Abercrombie, Second U. S. Infantry. This is the place visited by me in November, 1884, since which time the entire absence of change marks the truly conservative spirit of the village.

The only white man, the trader, Mr. Holt, informed me before landing that the Copper River natives had not yet been to the store to trade, but that they were in the Indian villages near the mouth of Copper River, and that he was daily expecting them. This seemed to partially prove that the ice had not yet gone out of the Copper River. The natives who had brought the report concerning Copper River natives (whom I will in the future call *Midnóoskies*, a Russian word meaning people of the Copper River) were not unanimous concerning the existence of ice in the Copper River. Some said that through fear of losing the ice upon which they traveled the Midnóoskies had returned without visiting Núchek; others that they had decided to wait until the ice went out, and until a May trading party had come down the river in a baidárra (skin boat). Either one of these stories might have accounted for their delay in bringing over their furs, but neither was correct.

I will say in the beginning of this report that information from natives has generally proved about as accurate as the above. Their conclusions from concomitant circumstances are so much at variance with those naturally reached by an educated mind that no confidence can be placed in them. Information, while wholly false, may not be prompted by maliciousness, but frequently is the result of inability to make proper deductions. They tell most wonderful stories about parts of the country with which they are unacquainted, and doubtless believe very much of what they say. These characteristics were found to exist among all the natives of the interior as well as along the coast.

After landing at Núchek on the afternoon of March 19, immediate
S. Ex. 125——3

preparations were begun for departure the following morning. To get transportation to Alagánik was not an easy task. The season for hunting the sea-otter was at hand, and the trader was making every effort to start the male population of the village on the hunt. Nearly all of these were accountable to the Alaska Commercial Company for liabilities incurred during the existence of the Northwest Fur and Trading Company's station at Núchek. The accounts due the latter company had been transferred and it was made incumbent on the present trader to collect them.

The natives, yet mindful of the Russian chastisements, obey through fear the present agent, who turns to advantage the presence of any vessel that is sighted or touches at Nuchek. The visit of the *Pinta*, fourth rate man-of-war, with her small armament, though not seen by any natives above mouth of Copper River, was the indirect cause of much respect shown us by the natives. The farther we ascended the river the larger became this vessel and its guns. At one place its length, as estimated by a man, was equal to the distance between two islands, approximately half a mile, and the bore of the guns was expressed by the greatest partial inclosure formed by the arms, tips of fingers widely separated.

After much discussion we finally obtained two row-boats, each with capacity of about a ton, exclusive of the crews, and three natives, two of whom were boys, the third an old man, who was to act as pilot. None of these natives were fitted for sea-otter hunting, hence their transfer to us. Had the circumstances not required immediate action, I should have delayed in order to get thoroughly able-bodied men. Knowing how destructive a few warm days, even in that latitude, are to bodies of ice, I decided to accept that assistance that would give earliest action and a start. In this as in all subsequent transactions with Alaskan natives the difficulty of a start was present.

At this place I engaged the services of Peder Johnson, a prospector, who had been employed by Lieutenant Abercrombie, and whose partner, John Bremner, had ascended the Copper River in a baidárra with the Midnóoskies in July, 1884. He was expecting news from Bremner which would decide his movements, but not hearing anything, agreed to accompany us rather than wait for the Midnóoskies to reach Nuchek.

I.—Nuchek in September.

NARRATIVE OF THE COPPER RIVER.

NUCHEK TO ALAGANIK.

On the morning of March 20 we left Nuchek for the mouth of Copper River in the two boats obtained from the natives, with crews consisting of four white men and three natives.

The three Eyaks who had informed us that the Midnóoskies were at their village, and who were on a trading expedition, had promised us assistance, but deserted us just as we were starting. They helped us in launching the boats in the heavy surf that was rolling on the beach, and promised us to jump in at the proper time, two in one boat, one in the other, but they failed to do so without giving any reason. To have returned for re-enforcement after the experiment we had had in launching would have been hardly advisable, inasmuch as breakers were rapidly increasing. The natives told us positively, as did the trader, that we could not launch our boats.

By the time we turned the southwest point of Hinchinbrook Island the breakers were washing our stores in the boats, and the natives insisted on returning to wait until the wind had subsided. The sun was yet shining, revealing with its splendor one of the finest water views along the coast, Prince William's Sound, surrounded on all sides with snow-capped and glacier-bedecked mountains. The face of Hinchinbrook Island on western side showed some remarkable folding of strata.

We continued our struggle. At 5 o'clock, having passed Johnstone's Point, we went into camp on the north side of the island, in a long, narrow inlet, where we found two deserted barábarras. The old native selected this as a safe harbor, prophesying at the same time the near approach of a storm. The "old man's" prophecy was fulfilled, for barely had we hauled up the boats and made them fast than it began to sleet and rain, nor did we see the sun from that evening until we had passed the limit of great precipitation, north of the Copper River glaciers. The dimensions of the barábarras here were about 8 by 10 feet, and about 6½ feet high, built in the same manner as those at Núchek.

The following day we left camp at 4 o'clock a. m., and passed through the narrow and shallow channel between Hawkins Island and the most northerly point of Hinchinbrook Island. From the southern extremity of Hawkins Island the storm forced us to direct our canoe to Point Whitshed, which should have been passed 2 miles to port.   Here we went into a small cove on west side of Point Whitshed, to interview an old native and his wife (Eyaks), whom we found by chance engaged in stringing clams.   From them we learned that there was no other "harbor" for our boat short of the mouth of Copper River, unless we ran up into the Eyak, several miles north of our direct course.   They spoke much of the mud flats, which we afterwards became acquainted with through sad experience.

I relied much upon assistance from the Midnóoskies, whom the Eyaks said had been at their village, Eyak, and who had a letter from John Bremner at Tarál to Peder Johnson.   Having worked continuously at the oars from 4 a. m. until 6 p. m., and being unwilling to pass the village of Eyak without information more definite than we could obtain from the two natives we had met, I decided to camp in the small cove.

Point Whitshed is a low, wooded peninsula, presenting a cragged appearance to the sea, and reaching within about 5 miles of Point Bentinck.   This intermediate 5 miles has been described by Johnstone as "a low, uninterrupted, barren sand as far as the eye could reach." I did not find it to be such, but rather an extensive flat of bluish yellow mud, covered with water during the stormy days of our stay at flood tide; but at low tide no water, as far as the eye could reach, could be seen.   These mud flats showed a network of tracks made by the small dugouts (canoes) used by the coast natives in their transportation.   These draw only a few inches of water, and along the flats when the tide is low are propelled by using the paddle as a pole. From Point Whitshed, looking to the southward and eastward, a long line of piled ice and dwarf trees marked the channel of Eyak River, extending out into the flats.

To reach the principal channel of Copper River, which we were to ascend in order to obtain water to float our boats, necessitated a start from Point Whitshed at 3 in the morning, about the time of flood tide.   The wind was dead ahead, from the southeast, producing a heavy surf, and darkness was supreme.   Our boats were constantly shipping water, yet for several hours we struggled against all difficulties, keeping close to the rugged and rocky shore, without a beach.   The more the tide fell the oftener we grounded on the mud. We had hoped to reach the channel of Copper River before this state of affairs could arrive.   Finally, as a means of economy, we tried to make headway by going out from the shore, but the tide was receding too fast and left us on the mud about eight hundred yards from shore.   A few provisions were then carried by us to the rocky shore over the soft, sticky mud, and were cooked with drift-wood found lodged among the rocks,

2.—In the delta of Copper River in the early fall.

Taking Pete (Peder Johnson), I started afoot for Eyak village, and after four and a half hours of tiresome walking over mud, ice, and snow, and sometimes through water, found a settlement of five houses, the dwellings of eight men, situated on the east bank of Eyak River, about one mile below the lake source of the same, and eight miles from the shore line of flood tide. Here we found the three Eyaks who had promised us assistance at Núchek, and learned that two of the Midnoóskies (called by them "Kinái") had been to Eyak, but had gone back to Alagánik by the portage; also that there was a letter for Pete, but its location was unknown. The fact of a letter having been sent down the Copper River was so unusual as to be a "topic of conversation" among them. These Eyaks could give us no satisfactory account of the ice on Copper River, some declaring it good, others contradicting them. While returning to camp in a small canoe with four Eyaks we hailed, when about 1½ miles from the shore line and just out of the channel of Eyak River, a canoe with a small piece of cotton cloth for sail. They were hugging the shore as closely as the shallowness of the water would permit, on account of the storm. One of the natives was "Skilly," a Midnoósky, and the other "Kawkus," of Alagánik; the former, "captain" of the Copper River party, the latter the most prominent man of his village. They had the Copper River furs in charge, and were *en route* to Núchek. Sighting their canoe seemed almost a godsend. They readily consented to sell their furs to me, and started for our boats, which we found could not be approached nearer than 200 or 300 yards, even in small canoes. We walked to the boats, thence to the shore, dragging our transportation over the soft mud, sinking in it in some places up to our knees.

Skilly promised (if we purchased his furs—$40 worth, Nuchek scale of prices) that he and three other Midnoóskies would give us assistance in our ascent of Copper River. He agreed to carry these back to Alagánik and there turn them over. It was indeed consoling that these upper river natives had not returned to their homes.

Of our reinforcement from Eyak, only two could possibly leave their "duty" to help us, and with these we prepared to start off again at flood tide. After wading out to our stores, we found the afternoon tide not high enough to float the boats, so were compelled to pass the night ashore, and leave at 3 a. m. the following day, when, after struggling against the head wind for two or three hours without success, the intense darkness making matters worse, we turned back to the camp on west side of Point Whitshed rather than be again left stranded on the mud flats. We arrived at the twice-used camp, and remained until the flood morning tide, when we again started for the mouth of Copper River, which we fortunately reached before the tide could drop us on the mud. Had we been half an hour later the same fate as that of the preceding day awaited us. We could only know that we were in the channel of the river by the "wind-row" of ice piled on its west bank. A divergence of a few yards either to right or left was sufficient to run the boats aground. As we ascended this western channel it became wider and the current stronger. The floating ice at times compelled us to entirely suspend rowing. We tried "cordelling," which was unsatisfactory on account of ice and numerous deep inlets along the banks.

About 7 p. m., after having rowed continuously for thirteen hours, we were stopped by an ice blockade. We had made our mid-day meal on hard bread in the boats. Had we been inclined to cook, the absence of timber of any description would have prevented it. As we were entering the mouth of Copper River, natives from the hunt, who had heard of our plans, began to assemble. Some of these had been seen by us off Hawkins Island. In their small canoes they found no difficulty in reaching Sákhalis in advance of us. At the proper place they carried their canoes up the muddy banks to the marshy flats, partly covered with ice and snow, and then made their way by foot to Sákhalis.

Our immediate objective was Alagánik, further up, and our supplies were not then so scanty as those of the natives; hence our dependence, unlike theirs, was water transportation. After reaching the blockade the stores were unloaded and piled on the muddy bank, with nothing to protect them from the mud and rain except the three tent-poles and the tent-fly. We had been exposed to the storm for four days; our clothes were completely saturated; some of us, too, had been in the water up to our necks, and here we were entirely without firewood.

Under the guidance of the "Old Man" and the Eyaks we started afoot for Sákhalis over this flat, barren of everything except swamp grass and a wonderful mixture of ice, snow, mud, and water, made worse by the continous rain and sleet of the past four days. Darkness was on us, and our little party of nine divided into three to try and find this village. After two hours' wandering it was found in a small "patch" of undergrowth, and consisted of two so-called houses, very small and equally crowded. These were each about 12 by 13 feet, and in the one where I slept were twenty-nine natives, ten dogs, and the household effects. The "Old Man" and one native strayed and were compelled to weather the storm without fire or shelter.

Here I was delighted to find two Midnoóskies, whom I employed, with all other available hands, to assist in transporting the supplies to Alagánik. The following morning great difficulty was experienced in getting the natives to leave the fire. On account of the packed ice our boats could be of no further service to us, and likewise the natives from Nuchek, who by this time were completely exhausted. The "Old Man" and his companion, that had strayed, appeared about 10 o'clock in the morning, just able to stand. We had not expected to see them again. We had employed them to go as far as Alagánik, but being by this time entirely useless, they were dismissed.

The stores were carried along the bank of the stream as far as a large slough from the west would permit and deposited in the mud, to be yet further damaged by the incessant, business-like rain. Some of the natives carried their packs about one-third the distance to the slough, deposited them, and returned to Sákhalis without even the ceremony of leave-taking. I gave up all hopes of getting the stores to Alagánik this day, so went thither (in a canoe which luck had seemed to place in our way) with Pete as interpreter. Before starting I had exacted a promise from the remaining natives to return on the morrow and give us assistance to Alagánik. I declined, contrary to their expectations, to reward them for their services until they had completed the task. We reached Alagánik at dark, and found Kawkus and Skilly, who seemed wholly unable to appreciate our hurry; nor could they give us any information concerning the condition of the ice on the river above. At this point there was no ice, but I attributed it to the effect of the tide, which was appreciable. At this village were only five men, all of whom I engaged, and started down the river in canoes the following morning to the stores. Between the point of first landing of stores and the slough were two ice-gorges, so that the first "deposit" required another portage before it could be placed in canoes. Of course, those at the slough had also to be carried quite a distance. By using all the available natives of the two villages, and by the diligent work of my party, the stores were finally landed at Alagánik on March 27.

Since the evening of departure from Nuchek, March 20, we had beencontinually exposed to sleet and rain, driven by strong southeast wind, which rendered the limbs numb and action at times almost impossible. On one occasion each of the party tried to light a match, but all failed on account of numbness and moisture. These days were severe ones, but an excellent discipline for the even more trying work that was soon to follow.

Though nearly all the inhabitants of Sakhalis had moved up to Alagánik, only six men were then available for our purposes. These promised one hour to go, the next refused all connection with the expedition. In order to persuade them that it was a great privilege I was extending, I decided to take only five, and had them draw lots to determine the one that was to remain. This had the desired effect, though I would gladly have employed ten instead of five.

The Midnóoskies, four men and a woman, Skilly's following then at Alagánik, were also unwilling to start in the rain. Several times they promised to move, but when the time fixed arrived they had numerous excuses to explain their unwillingness to go on. The Midnóoskies told me at the last minute that they were not going back until the trading party of May arrived from above.   All agreed that there was no ice in the river anywhere, and that the small canoes were unfit for its ascent.   This was extremely exasperating.

Lieutenant Abercrombie says of the coast people: "These natives are inveterate liars, and were they not cowards we would stand a very indifferent prospect of exploring the country with their aid to any extent."

On the morning of the 28th, with a native, I went 4 miles up the river in a canoe, when we met a man returning, who informed us that he had been up many miles, and that there was no ice.

ALÁGÁNIK TO TÁRÁL.

After returning, I decided to make a start in canoes, carrying sleds which could be used if ice were found.   Private Fickett was to be left behind with most of the stores, with orders to join us at Tarál in May or June, when the Copper River natives would be returning.   Two Midnóoskies were induced to help us.   On the morning of the 29th, the party, consisting of three white men, Sergeant Robertson, Peder Johnson, and myself, five coast natives, and two Midnóoskies, started in five canoes, carrying two men and about two hundred pounds of provisions and baggage each.   With this last were sleds and snow-shoes.

After an ascent of 6 miles up the river, NNE., the channel became too shallow for navigation, and a portage was necessitated.   This brought us to another channel, partly covered with ice, and here the sleds were first used.   Two canoes were carried across the portage and utilized on the water on top of the ice.   There was very little snow at this point, so that we were able to carry large loads on the sleds. Sergeant Robertson was sent back for other sleds and more flour. Pete was finally sent back for Fickett, with instructions to bring forward all the provisions possible.   At first this method of transportation seemed very favorable, but the continued increase of depth of soft snow made progress very difficult.   Fickett left Alagánik with Pete and one Indian, in the afternoon, but did not reach camp until daylight the following morning.   On his sled were about 450 pounds of supplies, with which they struggled to camp.   The rains had made the snow so soft that most of the time the top strips of the sleds were on the snow, and at times sleds and provisions were below the surface. Our transportation now consisted of six sleds, three similar to those used by the miners of the Stickeen River, one a native sled, and two made by cutting a canoe in two parts and then sloping off the tops from bow and stern respectively, thus making a kind of toboggan. It was soon evident that the greatest amount the best sleds would carry and make headway was 150 pounds.   Even with this they would break through the soft snow.

7.—Start from Alagánik.

3.—SOUTHERN PART OF CHILDS GLACIER.

On the morning of the 30th of March we abandoned about one-half of our ammunition, cooking outfit, food, clothing, &c. A few hours later we abandoned our tent and more clothing and food, and then had with us about 150 pounds of flour, 100 pounds of beans, 40 pounds of rice, two sides of bacon, 15 pounds of tea, some Liebig's extract of beef, deviled ham, and chocolate. The three Midnóoskies who had remained at Alagánik now joined us, but could give very little assistance on account of their own loads. A pack of 50 pounds on the back was, under the circumstances, as much as the strongest man could carry. In consequence of the water flowing over the ice, it became necessary to frequently cross from one side of the river to the opposite bank and to go from one channel to another. On two occasions we were compelled to improvise a bridge of drift timber to cross some of the channels, and frequently all our stores were dragged through water up to our hips. Our camps, without tentage of any description save our ponchos, on such snow as then existed, with an incessant precipitation of rain or sleet driven by strong wind, for discomfort beggars description. It was impossible to dry our clothes, a fact that one and all soon recognized, and while we hugged the fire closely, it was principally to fry a piece of bacon or bake a "flap-jack" (griddle-cake), operations in which we all took part. As soon as the meal was completed each sought his blankets and in a few minutes was fast asleep, though bedding and clothes were saturated.

On the night of the 31st of March we camped on the east bank of the east channel, opposite a point midway between two glaciers, one of which the natives say unites with the northern extremity of Sheridan's Glacier; the other, they say, heads near Eyak Lake. The most northerly of these two was called Goodman's Glacier by Lieutenant Abercrombie (to whom I am indebted for photography of Copper River below cañon of his name), and is only 3 or 4 miles below the southern point of Child's Glacier.

Lieutenant Abercrombie's description of Copper River as seen in July at this place is as follows:

Crossed the river and commenced the ascent of the mountain range on our left flank, which is from 2,500 to 3,000 feet in altitude. In the afternoon we came to a perpendicular wall, which forbade further ascent, but we had gained a sufficient altitude to see, far to the northeast, a high wall of ice, visible as far back as the eye (aided with a field glass) could see. To the north and almost joining the glacier on the northeast, we saw another monster moving off to the northeast. In our front, or east, lay a collection of thousands of small islands, covered as before described, varying from one-sixteenth of an acre to fifty acres in size, surrounded by a light-gray liquid, varying in breadth from a mile to a small stream, and in depth being about 3 feet here and about 18 inches further down. This was Copper River, that we thought might be ascended in a steamer for 50 or 100 miles!

On the morning of April 1 we left camp with the storm more severe than ever, the precipitation having changed to snow. Remarks about the day of the month, surroundings, and ourselves were in order. After crossing the river twice, we began the portage over the huge deposit directly opposite Child's Glacier, the condition of the ice in front of this forbidding an attempt along the river. This deposit was considerably elevated above the river-bed, and overgrown with small timber, which was so thick as to be a great impediment to the movement of our sleds.

Child's Glacier marks the first point in the ascent of Copper River at which only a single channel exists. From this point down the river varies in width from half a mile to fifteen between extreme channels. On my map I have, as far up as the glaciers, largely followed Lieutenant Abercrombie, but to claim that this delta mouth is accurately mapped would be a great assumption.

At Child's Glacier the river has a decided easterly course to Miles' Glacier, which is just north of the "portage deposit," and from it resumes its northerly course. The river between Child's Glacier and this deposit is about 125 yards in width, but just north of this and west of Miles' Glacier the bed is approximately 800 yards wide, with several channels studded with huge, well-worn bowlders or slickensides.

On the night of April 2 we went into camp on an enormous pile of immense rocks, heaped up in the center of the river-bed. On the east side of these was a very small and narrow channel; on the west the width does not exceed 50 yards; and this is Copper River. Its depth must be great, though the ice forbade our march over it and consequently any attempt to determine it. I have called this remarkable gorge "Abercrombie's Cañon." A few miles below this place Lieutenant Abercrombie describes the river as follows:

The river here narrows down to 150 yards from edge to edge of water, the difference in summer and fall being 20 yards. The spring rise is more than 40 feet, and the current runs from 10 to 15 miles an hour in the center of the stream at high water. This unusual rate causes a swash that throws the water up the rocky bank 10 or 15 feet, and the receding water carries every comparatively light obstacle, that is, bowlders weighing 700 or 800 pounds, back into the river.

The season of the year prevented our seeing such phenomena, though the swiftness of the running current was attested by the jamming and piling of ice 3 to 4 feet in thickness, the river above being yet closed.

Every morning before leaving camp I had the same scene with the natives, who were loath to leave their *forms*, and protested that we could not go farther. On the morning of the 3d day of April, after a terrible night, so reluctant were they to leave that I was compelled to pull down the small pieces of shelter they had erected and drag each one from his resting place onto the snow.

Our only fuel at the "rocky camp" was a very limited amount of drift-wood. No place in it could be found which would permit us

4.—Northern part of Childs Glacier.

5.—MILESGLACIER.

6.—ABERCROMBIE CAÑON.

to lie at full length, so our night was passed on our haunches, in a severe storm of snow and rain. At this time we had not learned to sleep "doubled up," as do the natives, and if we had the storm would have prevented it. The result was a night of watching and longing for day, with clothes as thoroughly saturated as though we had slept in the river. The coast natives had, of course, suffered with the rest of us, and were for some time disposed to go south to their friends, rather than north among people whom they feared. We were expecting to find plenty of food—they knew better—at Taráł. Finally, all were started over the mass of huge rocks, covered with snow, most miserable for sleds, and worse for the motive power drawing them. At times it became necessary to take off the snow-shoes; then the probability of going down between large rocks every few steps could be readily determined. After an hour or two of this kind of work it was found necessary to make a portage of 400 yards along the west side of the rocks, next to the main channel, after which we again began sledding, and were soon without Abercrombie Cañon, and to our great delight the weather was partly clear. All were encouraged and worked with renewed zeal.

For the first 4 miles the course was due east, next 2 ENE. next NE., and we were at a second cañon or narrows, called by me Baird Cañon, in honor of Prof. S. F. Baird, of the Smithsonian Institute. We camped at this cañon on west side of river, near a pile of drift-wood, on snow 4 feet deep. At sunset a heavy snow-storm set in, which by morning had completely covered us. From this time forward our sleeping-bags, of linen, made waterproof, were very useful. Their length was $6\frac{1}{2}$ feet, and their circumference sufficient not to cramp the arms and body. There were holes at the top for the introduction of a gathering string. For use the blankets were adjusted in the bags, then the feet were inserted between the proper folds, and the body shoved in. Generally a poncho was pulled over the head of the "bed" in place of closing the bag. The 4th of April was the first day that we caught a glimpse of the sun from the time of our departure from Nuchek, March 20, and the first day or night that was free from a precipitation in some form.

The glaciers mark the change of climate between coast and interior. We hailed the sun with joy, not alone on account of personal comfort, but through a desire to secure observations for position. The camp at Baird's Cañon was at the foot of a vegetation-covered glacier which extended along the river for 6 or 7 miles. A short distance above the cañon the width of the river is 2 miles, with two small streams emptying into it on the east side. This widened part, or lake, extends about 6 miles. Twelve miles above Abercrombie's Cañon we obtained our first observations for latitude. At the "lake" the river has a width of about 1,000 yards, with high mountains on each side, and here the glacier system is practically passed. At the head, on the east bank, is a very prominent rocky point, which seems, when viewed from the south, to jut out into the river, but which really helps to inclose the lake-like river.

We now found the snow firmer than any we had passed, and early in the morning, while the freezing of the previous night still had its effect, would support the weight of the sleds. The snow on the river along the lake was 4½ feet deep. In order to make the most of this good snow we did not halt to cook a mid-day meal where we could have obtained some small green wood, but continued our journey, satisfying the appetite with some beans boiled the night before. Hoping to find wood, we marched until 10 p. m., by which time it had become very cold, and our snow-shoes were rendered worse than useless. The sun during the day had melted the snow considerably, and as it began to freeze again it would clog on the snow-shoes. All efforts to prevent this, by continually striking them on the sides with a stick carried for that purpose, failed. Without the snow-shoes every few steps would send us into the snow up to our hips. Some of the sleds did not reach camp until midnight, and so exhausted were the men drawing them that they were compelled to lie outstretched on the snow several times within a few hundred yards of camp.

Our labors, so severe thus far, were barely begun; yet at this time I felt the greatest satisfaction in knowing that the doubt of reaching Tarál by snow was eliminated. Had the party been delayed a week longer there would have been no possibility of seeing Tarál until after the ice had gone out, and in such an event the party would probably have been compelled to pass the winter of 1885–'86 in the interior of Alaska. Two days, or even one night, might have sufficed to put the river in such a state as to have caused this delay. As it was, we were compelled to bridge channels to cross them, and at one of these places one of my natives barely escaped by being fortunate enough to grasp the edge of the ice as he was being washed down.

Unable to obtain wood, we were compelled to exist on a half meal of beans from 6 a. m. of the 4th until 10 a. m. of the 5th. We had halted but six hours during that time. Exhaustion was preying severely on the party when we stopped to take a meal just north of the Tetáhená, a stream of considerable importance entering the river on the east, 14 miles north of Baird's Cañon. The Midnoóskies had informed us that this river *broke* earlier than the Copper, and that we would probably not be able to pass it. The Tasnuná flows *in* from the west side, about 3 miles to the north, and is much smaller, though the appearance from the south does not indicate it. The Copper River, near the junction, is 1½ or 2 miles wide.

On the ice of the Copper River, opposite the mouth of the Tetáhená, was water covered with ice about one inch thick. The Midnoóskies would not give us assistance over this, or even wait to show us the route they had taken. With the aid of a long stick we would punch through the thin ice to find the shallowest water, following the navigable channels as determined by this novel "lead-line." Some places, where the old ice was far below the new, were passed on hands and knees. With the stick we found that the Tetáhená had several channels at its mouth, some of which were entirely open in the center. The only point at which to pass it was several hundred yards from the land, for the nearer the shore the more open was the Tetáhená. The passing of it was very risky.

Having thoroughly satisfied our enforced hunger, and jubilant at having passed the Tetáhená, all left the mid-day halting place in joyful spirits. Freezing had made the snow and ice splendid, and for one and a half hours there was a running struggle to keep the lead. Occasionally the winning sled would go through the new ice, and the next, by making a detour, would take the lead. Sometimes ice that would permit rapid crossing broke when a passage was leisurely attempted.

After sunset we came to a grove of cottonwoods, which at the time seemed to end Copper River; but which afterwards was found to be on an old island, heavily covered with timber and snow to a depth of 4 feet. At "Cottonwood Camp" we passed the night, wondering what had become of Copper River. To the west of this island there appeared to be a very small channel, and to the east one very much smaller than the Copper River should be. After leaving camp the following morning and marching 4 miles, we came out of the woods and sighted Tasnuná River to the west of an island about 3 miles long and 800 feet high, which we had supposed to be the main land, and between which and our camp was the above-mentioned small channel. West of this island is probably the principal channel of Copper River, which was pointed out to us as the Tasnuná River when we were south of Cottonwood Camp. The place of our camp was doubtless part of the same large island.

At this time the eyes of the party, with the exception of Fickett's and the Midoóskies, were a source of serious trouble, the coast natives suffering worst. The eyes of the Midnoóskies were as clear and free from inflammation as on the day of the start from Alagánik. Several times I was compelled to bathe the eyes of the coast natives with warm water and apply some ointment before they could be opened after a night's sleep. Sometimes they were so much swollen that opening was impossible; at such times their owners must work behind the sleds. A free application of tea proved very beneficial. It is a rather remarkable fact that the coast natives should suffer more than the whites of the party. None of the former were exempt, while one of the latter was.

In hauling the sleds one man usually preceded and pulled by means of a long string or rope, fastened to the end of each runner, and then passed over his breast, while the second man followed pushing with a long stick. The rear man could steady the sled, or right it when upset. Sledding even under favorable circumstances is not such smooth work as is generally believed.

For several miles above and below Cottonwood Island the river-bed varies from one to two miles in width. Six miles above it a small river, with a glacier source, called Konsiná, enters from the west side. Fifteen miles from the southern end of Cottonwood Island the mountains again attain considerable height. The highest peak here was called by the natives Níkneh. Six miles farther on we halted for the night on a sand spit, near the mouth of a small stream, called by the natives Zéikhell. The general course of the river was, thus far, north.

On April 7 the course from the Zéikhell to a very high mountain, "Spirit Mountain," on the east bank, a distance of 14 miles, was as follows: 4 miles NNE.; 5 miles ENE.; 4 miles NNE. Near the end of the first course were four islands, varying in height and size, the largest having a length of about a mile and a height of 50 feet. These islands have been named in honor of Seréberinikoff, the unfortunate Creole, who lost his life at the hands of the inhabitants after having ascended the Copper River farther than any other man not native. These islands presented to us splendid examples of stratifications, the beginning of extensive faces of slate schist which characterize the river farther on.

All the party now began to realize how difficult it was to make headway and at the same time hunt for food; hence each one strove to husband the small quantity of such that remained. At this time we made the first attempt at eating the entrails of an animal—a por-cupine. They were not relished then as they were at a later stage. At the porcupine feast of the morning the coast natives took occasion to smear their faces with charcoal and ashes, a thing that attracted little notice at the time, and was not explained until we went into camp at the foot of Spirit Mountain. This was the highest mountain yet seen by us (2,900 feet above river-bed), and we supposed it to be Mount Wrangell. The coast people had some remarkable superstitions concerning it. Kawkus, the oldest of the coast natives, informed us that formerly much fire and smoke were emitted from the mountain, and that now terrific rumblings were at times heard, all the workings of a Mighty Spirit. Great alarm was manifested at every sound proceeding from that direction, and there were many, the result of snow slides. The following morning they were very loath to leave camp in the storm, which they attributed to the wrath of the "Mighty Spirit," notwithstanding we had been exposed to similar ones almost from the time we left Núchek. The eyes

9.—Wood's Cañon.

of nearly all were now the source of serious pain, and, singularly enough, more painful during a snow storm than when the sun was shining.

After the natives had again besmeared their faces we left camp, hoping to reach Tarál during the day; but after traveling until quite dark, went into camp at the northern end of Wood's Cañon, so called in honor of Col. H. Clay Wood, U. S. A.

The course during the day varied between NE. by N. and NNE., and the distance traveled was 13 miles.

Near the middle of the march the river commenced to grow narrower, until one of the most picturesque pieces of landscape I have ever seen —Wood's Cañon—was reached. This is about 2½ miles long, with vertical walls of basalt and slate from 100 to 500 feet high. Above the limit of the vertical wall the mountains tower yet higher. In places the river does not exceed 40 yards in width, and so zigzag is the cañon that in several of the chambers it is difficult to tell the course of the river or to see more than a few rods to the rear or forward. In the largest chamber the greatest breadth is about 70 yards; on the east face was an ice river 100 feet high, 30 feet wide, and so natural in appearance that it seemed to have flowed at one grand burst from the rugged gorge above. When in this vicinity the only exit at first glance seems to be in the direction of the ice river.

At the upper end of Wood's Cañon, 60 feet above the river-bed, was a welcome sight to our eyes — the first house we had seen since leaving Alagánik. This was a small spruce barábarra, about 11 feet by 14, and a fair specimen of the houses of the Copper River natives. To get into this it was necessary to crawl through an aperture about 2½ feet high and 2 feet wide, passing through a "storm-chamber" about 3 feet long. There were no persons at this house, but in the cache were a few half-spoiled dried fish, of which we made a meal. This place was evidently used as a fishing station during the summer season. We would probably have passed by without having seen it had our natives not known of its existence. Our first impression on visiting the house was that it had not been used for years, but subsequent developments showed us that it had been inhabited during the preceding season, and probably many seasons in the past. On one of the upright pieces of the barábarra, opposite the entrance (the usual place for interior decoration of a Midnoósky dwelling), were hieroglyphics, representing men and their actions, which our friends interpreted and enjoyed very much. They were surprised that we did not understand these, and our failure to do so afforded more evidence to them of their superiority over us. We were not aware that this was also a suburb of the far-famed Tarál, which we reached the following morning, 2½ miles farther up the river.

The ice in the cañon (Wood's) and above was very perilous. In many places our trail lay over detached pieces, some of which were on end, due to the jam. In one instance I saved myself from a cold and dangerous submersion by catching with my arms as I was going down.

Tarál, the metropolis of the Copper River country, was saluted by us, at the urgent request of our native friends, at a distance of about 400 yards. The natives had spoken very much of John, the prospector, and about whom they expressed fear lest famine had overtaken him. The answer to our salute of many rounds was a single shot, and finally, at the edge of the bluff above us, one man, one woman, and two children appeared. The man was John, certainly the most uncouth specimen of manhood that I had, up to that time, ever seen. He was a picture of wretchedness, destitution, and despair, suddenly rendered happy. John was reduced to a single round of powder, which he fired in answer to us, supposing that the long-absent natives were returning alone from Núchek. He had sent down some skins by them, and had expected them back four weeks earlier, with a liberal supply of ammunition. In the mean time he had been living on rabbits which he snared, with occasionally a piece of dried salmon as a luxury. He was shortening his belt one hole every other day. At one time he declared the rabbits to have been very scarce, and starvation staring him in the face, a fact that his diary recorded. Nowhere did I ever receive such a warm greeting as at Tarál from this naturally heroic specimen of manhood, then so depressed with hunger and destitution. After having satisfied himself and answered our many questions, he sat up or walked about the rest of the night. He had ascended the Copper River during the previous summer with the Midnóoskies in a baidárra, and had reached Tarál with about 300 pounds of provisions, which he claimed were stolen from the house while he was away prospecting for minerals. The Midnóoskies, unable to reach Tarál with their provisions and those of John, had dropped him and his at Tetahená, or Bremner River, to which place they afterward went back for him. He did not reach Tarál therefore until September, by which time the cold had set in and prospecting was soon rendered impossible. John is a practical miner, having had many years' experience. He was disposed to consider the prospects for minerals around Tarál of little value, though eager to visit the copper region situated somewhere on the Chittyná River, which empties into the Copper River 3 miles above.

We reached Tarál April 10, with 230 pounds of food, with which to subsist a party of five white men and a number of natives until the Yukon River was reached, if this was possible. Our stay was passed in drying clothing and provisions, taking observations for

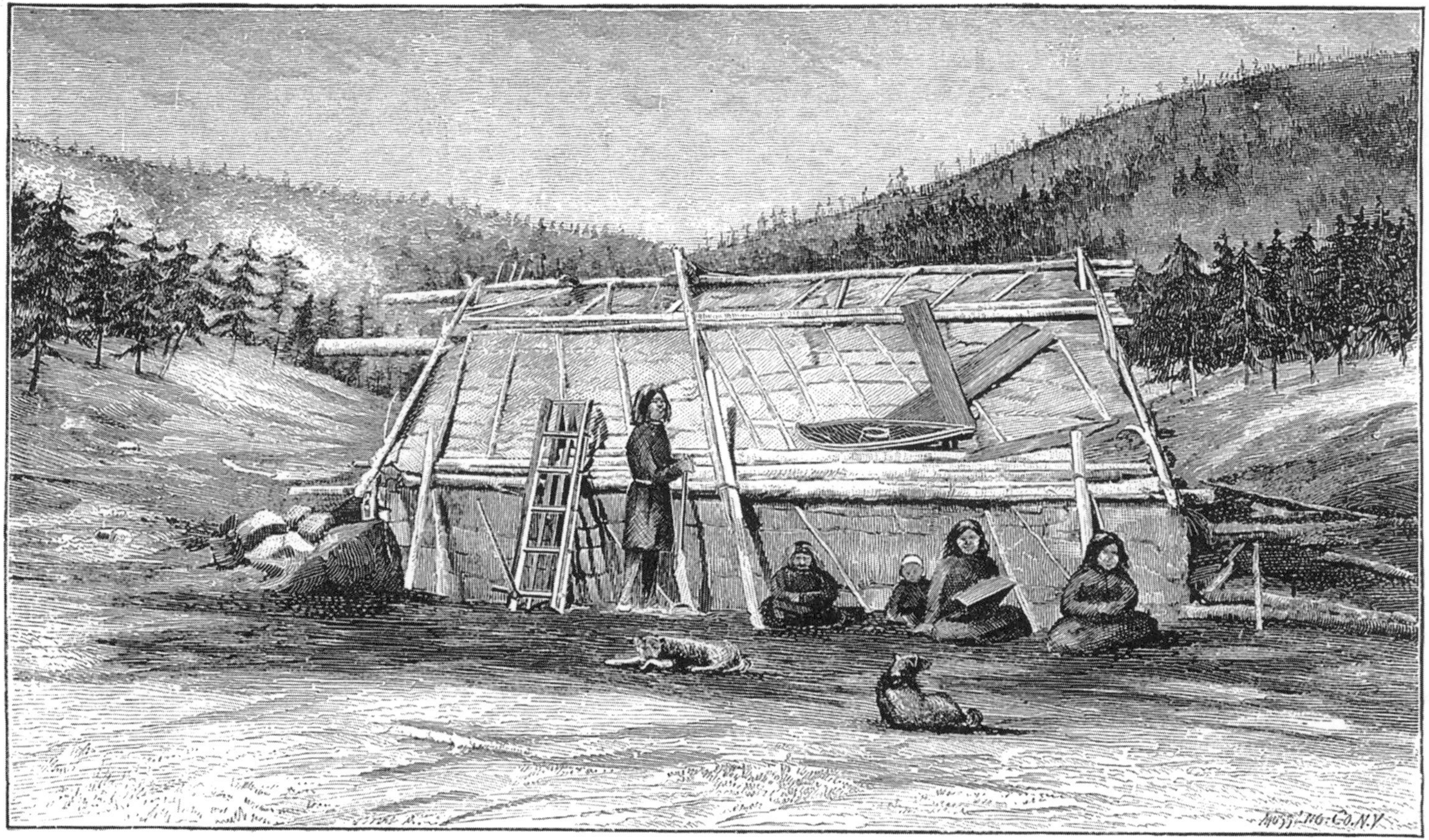

10.—Tarál.

latitude and longitude, and inspecting the nearest caches for dried salmon.

The condition of the river by this time rendered sledding no longer practicable; besides, I was unwilling to pass such an important tributary of the Copper River as the Chittyná without learning something about it and the supposed stores of minerals existing thereon. These reasons caused me to stop progress in the direction of the main stream.

The coast natives, who had reluctantly accompanied us thus far, were now dismissed, and with a few fish bones (the inward part of the fish, cured specially for dogs) set out for Alagánik, much thinner and more careworn than when first met by us. I considered their return perilous on account of the condition of the ice, a fact they realized. In speaking about it their faces would assume a pitiful expression; their worn-out moccasins and bloodshot eyes were alluded to. Altogether I felt much concern about their safe return, and promised each of them part of the abandoned rations for his individual use. This measure was probably useless in view of the attending circumstances. Letters were sent back to the department commander by these natives, informing him of our future movements as far as it was possible. These arrived at Vancouver Barracks, Washington Territory, in June, 1885.

The Midnoóskies who had accompanied us, excepting Wahnie, deserted us, one going up the Copper and two up the Chittyná.

We heard much of Nicolai, the proprieter of Tarál, Tyone of Chittyná, and chief trader among the natives, whom we had expected to find at Tarál, and for whose uncertain abode on the Chittyná we would soon start.

Tarál proper consisted of two houses, the one occupied by John, a winter house, and a summer house, at the time unused. John had constructed within the winter house a very small log hut made from the dwarf spruce timber which grows in the vicinity. At a distance of about 1½ miles from the winter house (Tarál) was a spruce bough tepee, rectangular in plan, used by several women and children. Slight traces of the Russian odinátschka yet remained, also part of a huge Greek Catholic cross. From this place the daring Seróberinikoff started May 16, 1848, never to return.

Our fish buyer returned late in the evening of second day after his start, bringing twenty-five dried salmon, all that could be obtained, though he was supplied with tea and tobacco, the most precious of luxuries to the Midnoóskies, with which to purchase them. Ten of these were given to the destitute women and children. Our effects, including 180 pounds of provisions, were *cached* at Tarál, and we left the following morning to explore the Chittyná River, with 22 pounds of flour, 25 of beans, 3 of bacon, a little tea, and 15 dried salmon,

ALONG THE CHITTYNÁ RIVER.

The party now consisted of five white men and one native. The packs were divided so that each man should carry an equal portion of baggage that was for the general welfare. An allowance of one blanket per man, a sleeping bag, or its equivalent, and a change of underwear was agreed upon for each. Carbines, pistols, ammunition, and cooking utensils were no small part of the weight. Any of the party was at liberty to carry articles of "luxury," provided he had also his allowance. One carried an extra blanket, another a coat or shirt.

From this time we began to realize the true meaning of the much-used expression "living upon the country." The provisions with which we started could easily have been consumed by us in four days, but they were held as a reserve. Our main dependence was on rabbits, the broth of which was thickened with a handful of flour.

The snow had nearly all disappeared on the river-bed and low-lands, and much of the journey was now over granitic bowlders and pebbles. Our feet were encased in native boots, and to persons unaccustomed to such footgear the use is a severe trial.

On April 13 we came up with Skilly, the Midnóosky, who would not wait and start with us from Tarál. He had parts of a moose that the wolves had killed during the winter.

The following is from Fickett's journal:

They had left a few scraps lying around, and these, that neither they nor their dogs would eat, we were forced by hunger to gather up and make a meal on. This is Lieutenant Allen's birthday, and he celebrated it by eating rotten moose meat.

If we had been so fortunate as to obtain even rotten moose meat a few days later there would have been none of the party too dainty to enjoy it. There were both snow and sunshine on the day of the 13th; on the night of the same day ice froze two-thirds of an inch in thickness. This cold was greeted with joy, because it enabled us to pursue a more direct course and permitted us to walk on the ice rather than the pebbles, a boon to our much swollen feet.

About noon of the 14th we passed three deserted houses on the south bank of the Chittyná, much concealed by a growth of cotton-woods and alders. Our camp was at the mouth of a small stream, reported to flow from a lake about 20 miles to the north of the Chittyná. This spot had been chosen as a camping-ground, and had a bath-house erected near the spruce-bough tepee. From here one of Skilly's subordinates started to the lake, where we were informed his mother lived. The name Skilly, by which we had known our native friend, I found to be a term applied to the near relatives of a chief. Our Skilly was a brother of Nicolai, whom we hoped to soon find, and upon whom great dependence for future assistance whilst on the Copper River was placed.

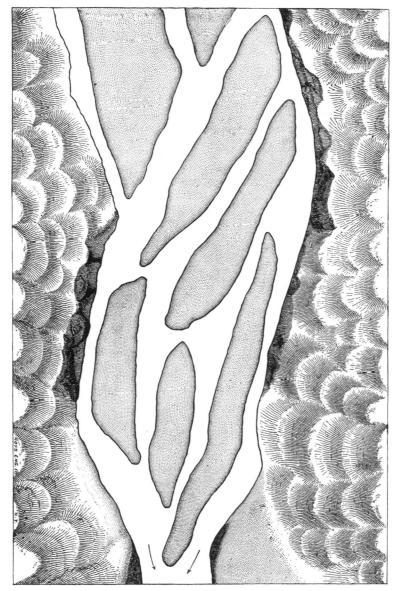

On the 15th we obtained observations for both latitude and longitude. To our camp, 30 miles from Tarál, the general direction was east southeast. We had passed through the slaty formation characteristic of Tarál above and below, and had reached a point where the northern bank of the river was steep, high, and of yellow clay, with traces of alkali. Notwithstanding the numerous bowlders and pebbles of granite in the bed of the river, no banks of the same material had yet been seen. The sun during the day had again loosened the ice in the river, and crossing it became very perilous. In an ordinary river such frequent crossings would not have been necessary, but in rivers similar to the Copper or Chittyná to follow a channel, if it were possible, would be to add from 30 to 40 per cent. to the distance. The beds of these rivers and their tributaries are frequently 1 mile wide, with several channels.

Near the end of the day's march found us with deep, impassable water to our front and right, and a very high, rugged point to our front and left. To climb this when in good physical condition, without packs or guns, would have been a difficult task. To cross it under the circumstances severely tested both the courage and strength of the party. The most difficult of all our endeavors, however, was the necessity of hunting supper at the expiration of such a day's march. Sometimes a halt was made during midday to hunt food for supper.

On the 17th we started at 7 a. m. from the mouth of the Chittyná, which bore no signs of breaking up, and having marched 5 miles, went into camp. The following is from Fickett's journal:

Rotten moose meat would be a delicacy now. So weak from hunger that we had to stop at noon to hunt. All so weak that we were dizzy. and would stagger like drunken men.

Fortunately, an old woman brought into camp a small piece of meat and a moose's nose, which, with the rabbits we killed, considerably strengthened us. The old woman was Wahnie's mother, who was in camp a few miles from the river. The latter, while out hunting, had gone to her brush house and told her to bring over the meat. She reluctantly obeyed, crying in a plaintive voice, "Skunkái descháne keelán" ("My children are very hungry").

The hunting party, for such it was we were near, consisted of two men, two women, and a number of children. They had been very unsuccessful in hunting, and were accordingly in reduced circumstances; yet we obtained of them a little meat. Our importunities for more were silenced by the verification of the old woman's sentence.

One of the men of the party was a "skilly"; the other unfitted by age for carrying a pack. From them I learned that Nicolai was on the headwaters of the Chittystone, near the mouth of which we had camped the previous day. At one time they would tell us that Nicolai had "Tenáyga keelán" ("Moose plenty"), at another that

"Nicolai deschéne keelán" ("Nicolai is very hungry"). At this camp
the skilly, who had been with us at times since our start in canoes
from Alagánik, left us to go to his house on the central fork of the
Chittyná, at a distance of 1½ *suns*. Upon the northern fork — the
Chittystone River, so called by us on account of the copper ore found
by the natives near it — was the home of Nicolai. The southern
fork, we were informed, was uninhabited, and must, from the reports of the natives and configuration of the country, have its source
a little to the north and west of Mount St. Elias. The central fork is
the principal one, or Chittyná River, and from Skilly's house to its
glacier source is 1 *sun*, making a total of 2½ *suns* from the confluence
of the Chittystone. From the confluence of the Chittystone to the
source of the southern fork is about 1½ *suns*. From our camp, 5
miles above the Chittystone's mouth, to Nicolai's house, via the portage, is also about 1½ *suns*. His house is near the glacier source of
the tributary. By the term *sun*, as used above, the Midnoóskies
mean a day's march. In making short marches the Midnoóskies, as
do most of the natives of the Tananá, travel with remarkable speed,
but they never load themselves with weight to exceed 20 pounds.
Generally they carry, besides a very light gun, only a skin blanket,
with dimensions of 4 by 5 feet. I do not refer to the men slaves,
who bear packs equal to those of the women. A day's march with
them is so very variable that we had no definite mode of arriving at
the distances to the sources of the tributaries except by reduction of
the time it required us to reach Nicolai's home; and using this as a
standard, I have traced in dotted lines the supposed courses of the
tributaries. Had I considered it prudent to attempt the source of
Central Fork, subsisting on rabbits alone, with no prospects of any
other food, the chart would not now show dotted lines. The party
was daily growing weaker on account of an insufficient quantity of
food.

The skilly of this camp, after much persuasion and rewards, was
induced to go with us to Nicolai's, but would carry nothing except
the "white tyone's" pack (mine). I was much degraded in his
eyes by carrying a pack of any description, and yet more so when I
shouldered the moose meat we had obtained from him. On April 18
we started overland for Nicolai's. For an hour our course lay along
the south bank of the Chittyná, then across it, over the treacherous
ice, to the north bank, into a wood of dwarf spruces and deep moss.
After an hour's marching through this we unexpectedly found ourselves on a high bank of the Chittyná, from which with the field
glasses we could see the locality pointed out to us as the junction of
the central and southern forks. The distance, in a right line, I estimated to be 20 miles. From this point the bearing of the junction
was SE. by S. and our course for the rest of the day was as nearly
constant as trail-travel can be, and was about E. 20 N.

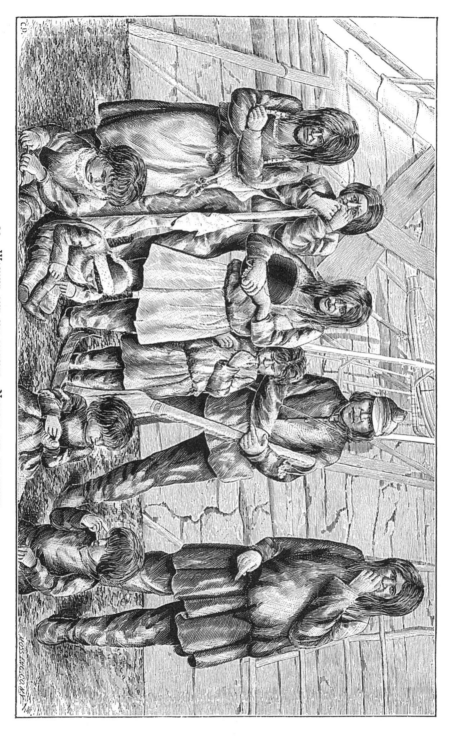

12.—Wahnie and his mother—Nicolai and his wives.

There was no trail and nothing to indicate the way save the blazing of the trees, which had evidently been done only a few weeks previous. When we halted for our noon meal a considerable quantity of the moose meat and two or three blue grouse were eaten, yet our hunger was not appeased. The skilly, soon after the halt, had fainted away, and remained in this condition during most of the meal. Wahnie felt much uneasiness concerning him, but most of the party seemed to realize the old maxim: " All is for the best." Certainly the portion of the meal intended for him was relished by us.

We left camp the following morning at 6 o'clock, and after marching about 7 miles found the strength of the entire party nearly exhausted. All of us now realized that a diet of meat alone should be very abundant to produce the necessary working strength. After consuming all the food on hand, we started off with the hopes that Nicolai would have something for us, and we were not disappointed.

The last 5 miles of our march was either on the ice of the Chittystone or very near the river. Many rounds of ammunition were fired by us in answer to Nicolai's salute. On occasions of this kind a Midnoósky will fire his last charge of powder, though hunger stare him in the face. It is courtesy that each shot be answered, and the number of shots with them, as with more civilized people, indicates the rank of the tyone. On one occasion, on the north side of the Alaskan Mountains, probably one hundred and fifty shots were fired to welcome us. Long before we had reached the source of Copper River, I was compelled to limit the number of shots, lest our supply of ammunition be too much reduced. We were always so delighted to arrive at a settlement that a celebration of some sort seemed very appropriate; moreover, it was claimed the greater the demonstration we made, the more food we would obtain.

It is also *en regle* among the natives to provide some kind of refreshments on the arrival of a guest, and we early learned to expect it as a matter of course. After having been once so entertained any subsequent meal must be purchased, and that at a very dear price. They realized our necessity and made the most of it.

To reach Nicolai's house we had marched a distance of 30 miles, and on finding on the fire a kettle with capacity of about 5 gallons, filled with meat, we were happy. The allowance of this per man, exclusive of the broth, of which we drank large quantities, could not have been less than 5 pounds. Much of it was fat or tallow run into the small intestines of the moose. All immediately fell asleep after eating, and on awakening were nearly as hungry as before. The donation of such a quantity of meat was frequently cited by Nicolai to show how great a tyone he was. More will be said of him, his people, and surroundings under the head of "Natives."

We soon examined the contents of the surrounding *caches*, and from our inspection of them concluded our guns must be largely depended upon to win us our food.

The 20th being stormy, the party rested, and gorged itself on moose, beaver, lynx, and rabbits, cooked entirely in native style, which does not reject in their preparation the entrails *in toto* of the last-named animals.

After much talking with Nicolai, he promised to make a baidárra of moose skins and go with us as far as Tarál, but would not agree to ascend the Copper River. On examining the river we found that the ice would not permit the use of a baidárra. Nicolai wanted to postpone the start for twenty days, but finally, through fear that we would go to Tarál before him, consented to begin the construction of the boat immediately. We were supposed to be in the heart of the mineral region, south of the Alaskan Mountains. This subject will receive attention further on.

While lying over at Nicolai's, awaiting the going out of the ice and the making of the baidárra, observations for position, hunting, repairing clothes, and making moccasins were the chief occupations. We found that the Chittystone had three forks, nearly equal in size, and that each one had a glacier source; that the principal mountain range, as seen from near one of these glaciers, makes an angle of about 30° with the general course of the river.

We were informed by Nicolai that tebáy (a variety of sheep, described under the heading "Animals") were plentiful; repeated attempts to obtain them resulted in two only being brought in during our stay. Rabbits were now, as heretofore, our chief support.

April 26 found Nicolai's "larder" nearly empty, and though the baidárra was about completed, a further postponement until the 28th was agreed upon to enable us to obtain some food. Fickett, Nicolai, and two natives started out with the intention of reaching the home of the tebáy and hunting on the 27th; but snow falling to the depth of 4 inches, and being accompanied by a strong wind, prevented hunting on the craggy peaks frequented by these animals.

On the 27th our host's two wives and four children started afoot over the trail we had so recently traveled. They were to be joined by us at the mouth of the Chittystone. On the 28th we started down the Chittystone River in our baidárra, covered with untanned moose skins. Its length was 27 feet, beam 5, and depth 22 inches. This boat was our only means of transportation from this time until May 31, when it was abandoned near the headwaters of the Copper River. It deserves a description. The framework, including keel, ribs, gunwale, &c., were constructed with no other tools than an ax and knives, which were of native manufacture. The assembling was done entirely by means of rawhide strings and willow sprouts. The seams in the cover were double sewed, and with sinew.

The skins, after being sewed, were placed in the river, where they remained several days prior to the stretching over the very flexible frame. The sewing is work allotted to the women, but an art in which the men are proficient. It would not be considered disgraceful for a man to sew, provided no woman is present; otherwise his self-respect would not permit him to use the awl and sinew. The skins were not in anywise cut to fit the boat; four skins were used; hence the boat contained three double seams. The fitting was due to the elasticity of the rawhide. This was made taut by rawhide thongs, passed successively through holes in the skins, then under the side pieces. The surplus skin at the bow and stern was folded so as to offer as little resistance as possible to the current, special care in this respect having been given to the bow. The boat, when completed, was very flexible and unsightly, but proved to be one of the hardiest small crafts I have ever seen.

The Chittystone, like the Chittyná and Copper, has in places a very wide bed, with numerous channels. Our boat, though flat-bottomed, grounded frequently, when it became necessary for all to step out into the channel and wade. During our first half day down the Chittystone we might have been designated as either a boating or wading party. Could all the channels of water, however, have been united there would have been no grounding. The current would easily average 6 miles per hour. The ice along the edges of the channel was from 4 to 6 feet thick, and largely the result of the solidification of snow. On one occasion, by holding to the rope, we permitted the boat to pass, stern forward, under an ice bridge.

Six miles below Nicolai's a small tributary of deep yellow color enters. Nicolai called it the Chittyto (Copper Water), and says that copper gives it its peculiar color, and causes the water to be so distasteful to salmon that they never ascend the stream. Its entire length is probably not more than 15 miles.

When 10 miles down the back bearing showed Nicolai's house to be due east. The run of the day was about 45 miles, though the right-line distance would probably not exceed 20 miles. From camp the back bearing to Nicolai's house was 5° south of east.

At night a snow of 2 or 3 inches fell, and Nicolai was loath to start the following morning, declaring during my conversation with him that a tyone should not be ordered. When he saw our stores loaded in his boat he sullenly decided to put in his property and accompany us. After a run of 25 miles in a torrent, most of which was through zigzag cañons, we were halted by ice, three-quarters of a mile from the Chittyná. During the run down the river our aristocratic companion, to his great pride, acted as captain of the crew and gave all directions, which could be abbreviated into three phases: "To Kwúl-le," "To Keelán," and "A-tó." The first means shallow water; the second, deep water; the third, paddle (verb). If the channel were difficult, in a loud voice he would repeat several times "A-tó." The shorter the turns and narrower the channel, the more necessary to have the speed of the boat exceed the rate of the current, a fact well known to our experienced captain.   Lessons in steering from Nicolai proved of great value in running the rapids of the Tananá, down which the natives could not be induced to go.

After having waited a few hours for the ice to go out, and realizing no advantage by our delay, we carried our boat and baggage to the north bank of the Chittyná, at its junction with the Chittystone, and went into camp.   At night we were joined by the two wives and several children of Nicolai, with their dogs, which were packed after the manner of a mule pack-train.   An investigation showed that the ice in the Chittyná would not allow the use of a boat, and a considerable delay seemed inevitable.   Several observations for longitude and latitude were taken at this camp.   In the afternoon a boat-load of natives, the ones we had seen at our last camp on the Chittyná before starting for Nicolai's, passed us, but were halted a few miles below by the ice.   At 3 p. m. we started out with the boat well loaded, carrying, besides our own party, two men, two women, five children, twelve dogs, and the worldly possessions of all.

After a descent of about 4 miles the ice forbade further progress. It was impossible to land on the south side, where timber was near; so we were compelled to carry our scanty bedding and camping effects 1 mile to a rabbit patch on the north side.   At camp we obtained quite a quantity of tombá, a peculiar variety of haw, that the storms of winter had not been able to beat off the bushes.

The following morning found us very hungry.   We were joined by the baidárra of natives and started down stream together, after having eaten the piece of meat obtained from the skilly.   This second boat, though not so large as ours, had equally as heavy a load.   Our *camarades de voyage* and our own party made a sight sufficiently picturesque to even call forth remarks from several of a party more interested in matters appealing to the stomach than to the mind.

The run of the day was about 22 miles, with a bearing varying from W. 25 S. to W. by N.   The ice having disappeared from the river, now revealed a swift current, averaging about 6 miles per hour.   The mountains facing the south were nearly cleared of snow to a line midway between timber line and summit.   Nearly all the snow and ice in the river-bed had disappeared.   The natives informed us that this river broke before the Copper, and started the ice below Tarál. A strong wind up the river lifted so much dust from the sand islands of the river that it was scarcely possible to see to steer.   On this river we also had occasional groundings.   The dust and a desire to again try for tebáy sent us into an early camp.

May 3 was passed in the camp, with the party suffering from severe pains across the loins. The rest at night was much broken by the frequent action of the kidneys.

The natives returned from the hunt with six tebáy, all of which were much smaller than the one John had killed. On May 4 we left camp, contrary to the wishes of our native friends, in quite a snowstorm, which turned into a rain towards the middle of the day. About 4 miles below camp we passed the mouth of a small stream that had not been seen when ascending. The natives informed us that there were tebáy on it, and I have called it Tebáy Creek. Four miles farther down we again passed the sweat-house camp, near the small river which I have called Dora Creek, in honor of a friend. General course during the day was a little north of west. The river possesses some very decided turns and many small rapids. At the junction of the Copper and Chittyná Rivers it is difficult to determine, when the channels are partially filled with ice, which is the largest. I was in doubt for a while as to which should be called Copper River, especially since the Indian name Chittyná means "Copper River." Subsequent events showed the western tributary to be much larger, and on this account I have continued it by the better known though improper name.

We reached Tarál late in the afternoon, to find our *cache* just as we had left it.

TARÁL TO THE TEZLINÁ RIVER.

The day after landing at Tarál was passed in writing letters, taking observations for position, taking photographs, and recuperating as much as possible on "white man's food." As usual, the natives were reluctant to start. Besides our own party we had Nicolai, Wahnie, and two other Indians. We now began work of a new kind, viz, cordelling, or tracking. Nicolai continued as steersman, and one other of the party remained in the bow with a long pole. The rest of the party pulled on the rope, which was about 150 feet long. We had not fully realized the strength of the current until now. A measurement showed a current of from 7 to 9 miles per hour. This velocity was obtained by measuring a distance along the bank, and observing the time required by a stick in passing over a corresponding portion of the river. The entire absence of canoes on Copper River is evidence of the swiftness of its current. The usual communication of the natives is afoot in ascending and by raft in descending. The baidárra is used for transportation to the trading station, Nuchek, and when an extended descent of the river is made. If it is used in ascending, it is always cordelled. The subject of "communication and transportation" is more fully given in another part.

One mile above the mouth of the Chittyná a torrent empties from the east side; from its mouth the bearing of Mount Wrangell is N.

10° E. From our camp, the home of an old man and his family, the bearing of the same is N. 20° E. From this time until the Yukon River was reached, we never failed to purchase or trade for all food the natives possessed, or would consent to let us have. At this old man's there was none. The settlement numbered nine in all.

At noon the next day we reached Messála's house, on the east bank, at the mouth of a small creek. Until within the past few years he had been head chief of the Atnatánas; but infirmity had deposed him, and left Conaguánta and Nicolai the principal men. He is the chief that led the natives in one of the Russian massacres, and manifested fear on my arrival, lest my mission had to do with him. After he had learned my business he seemed much easier, and wept at being able to offer us only half a dried salmon each. His face yet bears the characteristics of a man well fitted to rule. Both he and his wife are blind.

From the first camp above Tarál (Camp No. 1) to Messala's the general course is N. by W., with two rather marked curves; from Messala's to Camp 2, at an Indian house, the course is NW. ½° W. and about 6 miles. Vegetation had now begun to respond to the spring sun, and the "Natural Terraces" just below Camp 2, with their greenish grass covering, were a pleasing sight. These terraces present the same appearance as would the front of a huge earth fortification. The uniformity of the two slopes, one above the other, the uniform height of each parapet for several hundred yards, would seem to indicate the work of man rather than that of nature. At the camp a single woman was the only inhabitant, her husband having gone on a hunt. Camp No. 3, 7 miles farther up the river, four of these lying in direction W. ½° N., three NNW., was just above Konsiná Creek, a small stream emptying on the west side.

Camp No. 4 found us at Liebigstag's settlement, the most populous one yet met, numbering 30, including men, women, and children. Liebigstag, the Tyone of this settlement, is nearly an equal in rank to Nicolai, though not nearly such a diplomat. A part of his constituency is on the flat on the east bank, just above the torrent stream flowing into the river almost directly from the northern base of Mount Wrangell. His summer headquarters was on the west bank, on the very edge of a bluff 600 feet high, as determined by a barometer. From our camp on the flat we could barely hear the reports of guns fired as a salute to us. Our approach had been heralded by two men whom we had met a number of miles down the river. These acknowledged allegiance to Liebigstag, and considered it their duty to immediately change their plans, return, and inform their sovereign of such a previously unknown event. Seréberinikoff possessed the most Caucasian blood of any one that had ever visited these regions. We were invited to Liebigstag's house on the bluff. To cross and recross the river here was no easy task, yet Fickett and myself, with Nicolai

Mt. Sanford.   Mt. Drum, 13,300 ft.   Mt. Tillman, 16,600 ft.   Mt. Wrangell. 17,500 ft.

Mt. Blackburn, 12,500 ft.

14.—CREST OF RANGE AS SEEN FROM LIEBIGSTAG'S.

and several natives, attended the feast, and a bountiful one it was. Never have I known lines of caste to be so rigidly drawn as with these people. I was considered the chief, and in ascending the bluff, natives had come down to escort us up and carry my bed. Two half-grown boys preceded to the summit, then took station on each side of the trail till I had passed between them and had entered the spruce-bough tepee. There I found all allotted places according to rank; Liebigstag and blood relatives on the right side, "retainers to camp" on the left. Places on his left and right respectively were reserved for Nicolai and myself. Fickett was assigned a place with the 'oi polloi.

I did not have time nor was it in my instructions to attempt any reform in their social or political customs; yet had we been less dependent on the natives I should certainly have let them understand that the ablest worker was the chiefest man, rather than continually make presents to the recognized tyones. On one occasion, when I attempted to snub a lazy chief by making a much-prized present to one of his vassals, and a splended worker, rather than to himself, he pocketed the article and took all credit to himself for possessing so valuable a worker. These tyones barely condescended to consider me their equal, and on no occasion would they consider my men as such. They were reluctant to believe that any one who would pull on the rope of a boat, carry a pack, or take equal foot with his men could be a tyone. At this camp we obtained a considerable quantity of meat and quite a following of natives to pull on the boat and hunt. From Liebigstag's camp is one of the finest views I have ever seen. The mountains to the east and north of the river are grand. The most southerly of the prominent peaks is due east, and has been called by me Mount Blackburn, in honor of Hon. J. C. S. Blackburn, of Kentucky. Its elevation above the river is about 12,500 feet. The bearing of Mount Wrangell from same is NE. $\frac{1}{2}°$ E., and has an elevation of about 17,500 feet. The next peak above, called by me Mount Tillman, in honor of Prof. S. E. Tillman, of the United States Military Academy, is about 16,600 feet high, and probably ranks third in height among the peaks of North America. The next is Mount Drum, 13,000 feet above the sea-level, called in honor of the Adjutant-General of the Army. The last prominent peak, barely visible from the same point, has been called Mount Sanford, and is 12,500 feet in height. The determinations of the heights of these peaks did not involve the rotundity of the earth, but simply the solution of plane triangles, hence cannot be accurate. Frequent compass bearings of them, taken as we ascended the river, also the vertical angles with the sextant from the same points, furnished the data for the determination of height and position. A reasonable approxima-· tion is all that is claimed. The accompanying sketch shows the mountains, including the high peaks. Looking to the north was

Copper River, with its numerous gravel islands and channels, with plenty of ice in it both packed and floating as yet. Between Mount Wrangell and the river are three ranges of mountains, one of which was snow-covered, thus proving its elevation to be considerable. Along this part of the river absence of rocks characterizes the banks. These are very variable in height, and chiefly of recent sedimentary deposit. There is splendid grass near the river, and the flat opposite Liebigstag's had the appearance of an excellent stock range. It was sufficiently elevated to be dry, and was partially timbered with cottonwoods and spruces.

After exposing a number of photographic plates, the party started off with a liberal supply of moose meat, and as a consequence in excellent spirits. We now had seven natives to assist in cordelling, besides the two tyones and two hunters. With Liebigstag as captain, our chances for taking the most direct channel were much increased. Beyond this our first natives were little acquainted. For several days only two whites kept with the boat; the others followed the trail along the east bank of the river, which at times lay several miles away. The party following the trail was supposed to furnish game, but its efforts to do so were not very successful. An occasional goose or duck was killed in the river or a slough, but our chief dependence was rabbit.

After leaving Liebigstag's the river continued to bend westward, the general bearing being between NW. and NNW. On May 11 we sighted the small mountains that give rise to the stream on the west bank, called by the natives Klatená. These mountains are a continuation of the range to the west of the river, but are so low that very little snow was on them. From the same point Mount Wrangell, sending up a white smoke or vapor, bore E. 25 N. After one of the longest day's marches while cordelling, we went into camp about twenty miles above Liebigstag's, from which camp Mount Wrangell bore E. 12° N. and Mount Drum N. 30° E. From Camp 5 to mountain behind Tarál the bearing was SE. ½° S.

On the 12th we traveled 6 miles W. ½° N., then 3 miles WNW., and went into camp one mile above Conaquánta's winter house. He and his immediate family were out in a hunting camp, but our halt was with a band of his followers, all of whom were arrayed in their best to welcome us. Our approach was, as usual, heralded several hours in advance, and it had now become imperative on me to make an official visit to the ranking man of each settlement, however small. At this settlement, the most numerous on Copper River, were 23 men, 8 women, and 16 children. To our great surprise, we found a few pounds of flour and a few ounces each of tea and sugar, besides some fancy cups and saucers. The possession of the latter was an infallible index of Tyoneship in one of its grades. Their flour had come from Tasnai, which to this time we had been led to suppose was at the

15.—MOUNT WRANGELL.

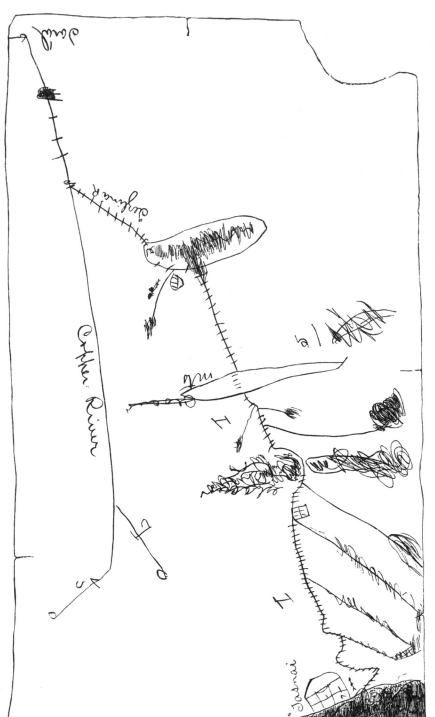

18.—Native map of the route to Cook's Inlet via the Suchitno River.

mouth of the Tananá River, but which in reality was the mouth of the Suchitno, in Cook's Inlet.

I had frequent maps made by the natives to show us the trail over the Alaskan Mountains and down the Tananá to the Yukon River, all of which indicated the route to be via the Tezliná River to Tasnai. The accompanying sketch represents one of the maps thus made. Since leaving the Chittystone we had been deluded into thinking we knew our course. The strong tendency of the river to the westward and the comparatively low latitude, as determined by our observations, awakened my suspicions, but it was not until we reached the Tezliná that I felt sure the trail up it could not lead over the Alaskan Mountains, but rather to Cook's Inlet.

Having obtained observations for position at camp, we left the following morning with but four natives—Nicolai, his two vassals, one of whom was Wahnie, and Chetoza, a vassal of Liebigstag, who had to be amply rewarded for permitting him to escort us. The assistance rendered us by the many natives recently with us was valuable, but their ceremonies and great sense of rank were very oppressive to my party. Nicolai, when with Tyones, was equal to or worse than any of them in this respect, but when with us only he was much more endurable. None of the natives would sell us food of any kind without consulting him, and he advised prices that would make a commissary in civilization shudder. They realized full well our dependence, and made the most of it. Instead of acceding to our terms, we were almost invariably compelled to yield to theirs.

At 1 mile from camp we passed two more unoccupied houses of Conaquánta, the best found on Copper River. Our course for 4 miles was NW., and for 3 NNW., when we went into camp No. 8.

The mean barometer reading while in camp was 28.67, which showed Camp 8 to be 750 feet above Tarál. Camp 9, at an estimated distance of 9 miles from Camp 8 by the channels of the river we followed, was, according to the barometer, 110 feet higher. This is not more than the average rise from Tarál northward, as will be seen by consulting the barometric table in the Meteorological Appendix. This wonderful fall of the river will account for the torrent-current which the Copper River has from its source down to the glaciers.

Midway between the camps we passed the mouth of the Klatená, the largest tributary of the Copper save the Chittyná yet passed, and a stream of size, as shown by the general topography of the country. The mountains on the west side, as far as the eye could reach, seemed to be separated by this river. Natives report this river to head near Nuchek in a large lake, where fish are abundant; that to reach Nuchek, however, would necessitate the crossing of large glaciers. Nicolai informed me that he had been to its source when he was a small boy. In accordance with his recollection I have traced it in dotted lines on the accompanying map.

One mile above the Klatená, on the east bank, enters the Klawasiná, a small tributary.

From Liebigstag's to Conaquánta the river varies from a half to a mile in width, with numerous channels. From the Klawasiná to the Tezliná the river is generally confined to a single channel, with decided curves.   During the march the bearing varied from NW. to N. 20° W.   After having exposed eight plates, the photographic instrument and all the plates exposed during the time on Copper River were carefully packed and *cached,* to be taken down to Nuchek by Nicolai on his return.

Camp 10, May 15, found us at the mouth of the Tezliná, where we bade good-bye to Nicolai after putting in his possession several letters descriptive of the journey to that point.   We had passed beyond the territory of the Atnatánas to the neutral grounds that separate them from the Tatlatáns.   We had to depend almost wholly on our own resources from this time forward.   *En route,* until the headwaters of the Copper were reached, we observed the greatest destitution and hunger within our experience in Alaska.

In my letter, sent back to the department commander, no information whatever could be given of our future movements.   No natives had been met who had ever heard of a trail over the mountains to the northward.   The Copper River here showed little or no diminution in volume.   The Tezliná, which we had expected to ascend, was little if any larger than the Klatená, and only about 25 or 30 yards wide, besides being swift, with a bed filled in with bowlders.

FROM THE TEZLINÁ RIVER TO LAKE SUSLÓTA.

The natives informed us that we had no chances of reaching the source of the Copper; that the current was so swift that to cordell the boat would be impossible.   They also spoke of the many channels, which we found to exist to such a number as to keep us almost continually in the water.

The buds of the cottonwoods were now partially opened, but the salmon would not arrive until the leaves had appeared and attained their full size.   Frequently we imagined that fish had struck our legs when wading across these many channels, but this sensation proved a delusion.   The ice was yet floating in the river, and the temperature of the water 43 Fahrenheit.   A day was passed at the mouth of the Tezliná to try and replenish our supplies by hunting, but without success save to the extent of a few rabbits.   Sergeant Robinson shot at and wounded a small black bear, the only large game seen save the tebáy of the Chittystone.

No buoyancy of spirit characterized the party as it left the mouth of the Tezliná, entirely in ignorance of what was in store for it; and, wearied with hunger and other hardships, there was just cause for melancholy.   The party had scarcely been dry day or night since leaving Tarál. During the day we had an accident which might easily have proved fatal to the success of the expedition. In crossing the river, an undertaking circumstances frequently necessitated, our skin boat struck and lodged in the middle of the channel, where the current was terrific, on a huge hidden bowlder. The dogs were thrown out of the boat, the sides of which were crushed in, and for a few minutes general consternation prevailed until we were again safe on land. Had the boat upset our bedding, guns, and instruments would have been lost, and doubtless the lives of some of the party. This event seemed to add no little to the general depression of the party.

Two miles above the mouth of the Tezliná the bearing of Mount Drum is E. 20° N. The course of the river during the day was nearly due north, with some very marked curves. From Camp 12 the bearings of Mounts Drum and Wrangell were respectively E. 10° N. and E. 13° N., with angles of elevation 3° 20′ and 5° 06′. The barometer read 28.05, showing camp to be 1,275 feet above Tarál and 1,850 feet above sea-level.

Before leaving camp, two runners from Conaquánta's hunting camp reached us with about two meals of moose meat, for which we traded.

The grass had now given way to the deep moss, which continued to characterize the country, with an occasional exception, throughout the remainder of our explorations. We left camp after repairing the baidárra, an operation that had become a daily necessity on account of the rottenness of its skin covering, produced by continual moisture.

One mile above camp, on an island, were springs so strongly impregnated with minerals that their waters could not be drunk. Even a sip left for a long time a disagreeable taste. The deposit on the gravel showed the presence of iron. We were unable to carry any of it away.

Three miles further up the mouth of the Tonkiná was passed. It showed a volume of water, the cross-section of which was about 30 feet by 3 feet.

Numerous channels necessitated almost continual wading, which was now seriously showing its ill effects on the party. Improper circulation of the blood and frequent discharge of urine at night was the cause of much sleeplessness. Ice froze in the cups to the thickness of half an inch during the night of May 20. The geese had begun to lay, however, and occasionally we could get one, with its eggs, of which there were never more than six.

Two miles above Camp 14 we passed the mouth of the Gakoná, so concealed by timbered lands as not to be visible. The diminution in volume of the Copper after passing this point showed this to be no inconsiderable tributary. The bearing up it from near the junction

Mt. Drum, E. 10° S., 13,300 ft.   M

16.—As seen from point s

E., 17,500 ft.   Mt. Tillman, SE. by E., 16,600 ft.

VE MOUTH OF GAKONA RIVER.

is NW. The positions of the various camps are shown on the accompanying maps.

Three miles below Camp 15 we obtained thirty salmon from a deserted *cache* in such a condition that our dogs hesitated to eat them, yet hunger compelled us to do so. On the 22d we went into camp early in order to replenish our "larder" by hunting, but had little success. A smoke far in advance seemed to promise something cheerful, but soon we found that the natives, whose presence it indicated, were traveling north as well as ourselves. From their trail we knew they had no boat, hence our chance of overtaking them was very indifferent. The river again appeared in a single channel, an unusual sight on the Copper.

On the 23d, at Camp 16, another effort was made to obtain large game. One party crossed the river towards the peaks on the east; the other hunted on the west bank. Neither of these obtained any game. The thoughts of all were now centered on the natives in advance whose smoke we had seen. From a high hill behind Camp 16 a great stretch of country was visible. Huge snow-capped mountains to the north and west, evidently the principal range south of the Tananá River, were seen for the first time. The highest visible peak of the range, which bore N. by E., I have called Mount Patten, in honor of Captain Patten, of the U. S. Q. M. D., though I have been unable to definitely locate it on the map for want of other observations of it. It was supposed that this peak was seen several times after reaching the Tananá, but the bearings when plotted do not agree. The farthest visible water of the Copper River bore ENE. Mounts Drum and Tillman bore respectively E. 15° S. and SE.

On the 24th we passed the first natives seen since May 15. They were the thinnest, hungriest people I have ever beheld. The children were slowly wasting away. Their only support had been a few small fish, rabbits, and roots. Their supply of food on our arrival contained roots only, but the men were off for fish. We examined not only the *caches*, but the contents of everything that might possibly contain food, with a view of satisfying our hunger, but to no purpose. This settlement was on a small tributary of the Copper, on the west bank. It was our intention to camp near them, but so pitiful was the sight that we marched 3 miles farther. Our condition was better than the natives—thanks to our guns and ammunition. I shudder to think of the subsequent condition of those poor women and children, unless the salmon-run quickly followed us.

The last 3 miles traveled were in the direction of NE. by E., and the river was 1½ miles wide. The water had risen to such a height that we were compelled in numerous places to cut the small timber, ordinarily a short distance from the water, to be able to cordell the boats. Our marches continued to grow shorter, in spite of strenuou efforts to prevent this.

From Camp 18, a high mountain, Mount Sanford, above Mount Drum, was seen for the first time since leaving Liebigstag's. Its bearing was E. 17° S., whilst Mount Drum bore SE. ½ S.

On the 26th the mouth of Sanford River, a torrent from the east, was passed.

From leaving one camp until making another, we were almost continually in the water, and a distance of 6 miles had now become a huge march, so difficult was the river and so worn the party. On the 27th we passed the mouth of Schnuna River, a torrent from the west, and went into camp, not having traveled more than 4 miles. The river had many turns at this latitude. I have refrained from detailing its course, which is shown by the map.

The size of the boat we now found to be too great for the strength of the party, and larger than necessary to carry our all, so, at Camp 20, Sergeant Robertson and Bremner remodeled and reduced it. Camp was near a native house, though the only native we saw was a cripple, who wanted permission to accompany us, claiming that he was a skilly, and related to the big Tyone of the Upper Copper. From him we learned that there was a trail over the Alaskan Mountains, but it was *kuteshit, kuteshit* (far, far away). He was willing however to go, but to subsist him would be necessary. We rejected his services, and supposed that this would be the last of him. Not so, however, for he continued to follow along the woods, always appearing at meals, whenever we halted on the side of the river on which he was. After a while we found that he could be a valuable assistant, by digging roots, and he was added to the party. He proved a genuine skilly, in fact a Mascot, without whose services we would undoubtedly have suffered much more than we did. Even rabbits were now difficult to obtain, and the little flour and rice kept back for moral effect were now used to appease our hunger.

The following is from Fickett's journal:

May 28.—Had a little paste, rotten and wormy meat for dinner; rotten goose eggs and a little rice for supper. Each meal about one-fourth of what we needed. We went into camp. Whole party played out.

May 29.—Party nearly played out for want of food. Can just crawl. Had to stop middle of p. m. to make a flap-jack for each and a little beef tea. Decided to abandon boat at the next Indian house.

May 30.—Temperature of water 43. Course NE. by E. Arrived at an Indian house at 11 a. m. hungry. Decided to abandon boat. Indian gave us a dinner of boiled meat, from which he scraped the maggots by handfuls before cutting it up. It tasted good, maggots and all.

On the morning of May 28 we passed the mouth of the Chitslétchiná. Its cañon for many miles bore N. 20° W., while the Copper bore N. 30° E. The two seemed nearly equal in size, and for some time I was in doubt as to which one to ascend. The cripple decided me, by saying that there were no natives on the former, but there were some on the latter. The trail over the mountains was yet very indeterminate, the cripple having informed us that two moons would be required to make the portage. I thought perhaps a shorter route might be found from the head of the Chitslétchiná, the mouth of which had several channels, separated by thick ice resting on the gravel bars.

A few miles above the junction of the rivers we reached a camp of natives, twenty-three in number, all ready to start for Tarál for the fishing season. They did not contemplate a return until the following winter. Here the Copper was again in a single channel, and showed itself a much smaller river, its width being only about 100 yards.

On May 30, after a march of 3 miles, we reached a native settlement of four souls (Camp 22), and found the natives above the Tezliná. Here we abandoned the baidárra to take a portage, the chord of an arc represented by Copper River. At seven miles from camp the bearing of Mount Sanford was S. 5° E., and Mount Drum S. 20° W. Noon observation showed us to be in latitude 62' 54' N.

The Tatlatán cripple took the trail, and we followed in single file, with packs on our backs. Our three dogs were utilized for the first time as pack animals, and were of much value. Our guide was crippled to the extent of having a shriveled leg, for which he substituted a long stick that passed behind the shoulder and above the head when adjusted to assist walking. The lower end of his staff was broadened to prevent its sinking into the sphagnum; his speed and endurance seemed wonderful. Our trail, on June 1, lay closer to the river, and 3 miles from Camp 23 we crossed a clear stream of dimensions 30 feet wide by 1½ feet deep, which we knew to be a fish stream by the appearance of the camping-ground upon its bank, and the fish traps lying in and near the water. The house, usually found at such places, had been burnt, and no natives had stopped in the vicinity for many months.

On the banks of this stream, where the moss had been destroyed, was the luxuriant growth of grass that generally springs up near settlements. This fact may prove of value if it ever be considered prudent to attempt the cultivation of barley, or the hardy vegetables, in such high latitudes. The country over which we were traveling was covered with marshy lakes and a growth of dwarf spruces, both dead and alive, besides a fair quantity of cottonwoods. It differed in no material respect from the country of the Chittystone River, over which we portaged. The berry bushes (several varieties) were in bloom, and the foliage of the trees was nearly complete, indications that the salmon should be at hand.

Camp 24 was on the Copper River, which here has a course nearly due east and west. About 3 miles to the west of camp the Slaná River empties from the north. It is a tributary of considerable proportions, if we judge from the diminution of volume of the Copper above their confluence. From its source, Lake Mentásta, a trail also leads to the Tananá.

June 2 our course lay along the river, which now bore ENE. for several miles. Suddenly, to my surprise, the cripple began crossing some of its numerous channels. The bed of the river here is fully a mile wide, and there are probably ten channels, varying in depth, where we forded, from a few inches to 2½ feet. Between the channels are gravel and small bowlders, with an occasional island covered with willow. In fording these channels the party found it necessary, on account of the swiftness of the current, to join hands, thus proving of mutual assistance.

After crossing the river our course lay NE. for about 5 miles, over a well-worn trail, a pleasant sight to us. When within a mile or two of the Tyone's we passed a collection of snow-shoes and sleds placed in the branches of the trees. Why these articles should usually be stored at a distance from the house I was unable to learn, but such is the custom with all of the Copper River natives. The cripple had gone in advance to notify Batzulnéta, for such was the name of the chieftain, of our approach. The usual salute with guns was exchanged, and we were met by thirty-one men, ten women, and fifteen children, the latter, of course, in the background. Of these natives, quite a number were from Tananá, and had gone into summer camp with Batzulnéta, to be ready for the run of salmon. That the Tananatánas should come to the Copper River to fish was very significant. Here there was but one winter house, and that occupied by the Tyone and his immediate following, while the other natives were living in spruce-bough houses. Batzulnéta, the largest native seen by us in the Territory, was 6 feet 4 inches high, and clad in a blouse of scarlet flannel, obtained from a trading station on the Yukon River, and a pair of native trousers, which included the foot gear. His shirt of cotton cloth, and a black woolen hat with strips of red flannel, completed his costume. His hair hung down his back in a tangled roll 3 feet long, showing no signs of ever having had any attention. As a medicine man, he could neither have it cut nor combed. Over each ear hung two small braids, secured at the ends by beads and sinew. Altogether he was the most picturesque character we had met, yet his face neither showed courage nor cunning. His ascendancy had doubtless arisen from his position as medicine man, possibly from a superstition concerning his unusual stature.

One of the natives from the Tananá made a map of the Yukon and Tananá, which is inserted to show how great is the geographical knowledge of these primitive people. He assured me he had been to the stations on the Yukon, at Fort Reliance and at Fetutlin, the former kept by Mr. McQuisten, the latter by Mr. Harper, both of whom we afterwards met on the Yukon, below the mouth of the

Tananá. He was entirely ignorant of their surnames, but spoke of "Jock." These natives, likewise those on the headwaters of the Tananá, call the Yukon River, Niga To; the White River, Natsiná; the Tananá, Nabesná, and by such names we spoke of them to the natives until we were two-thirds of the way down the Tananá.

At this camp we bade good by to Wahnie and Chetoza, both of whom were in a sad condition, due to the constant exposure and hardship. Each had contracted a severe cough, and both were very much reduced in flesh. Wahnie had become much attached to us, and wept at parting. Their services for the last few days had been of very little value. The usual meal was given us on our arrival, but after that food of any kind was difficult to obtain at any price.

The natives were hourly expecting the salmon, and would frequently go to the small river near by, and put in the dip-net. Inspired by their hopes, June 3 was passed in waiting, on a diet of half-rotton salmon and a few rabbits, the moose meat having been exhausted. During the afternoon of our arrival all the males (eight) from Lake Suslóta came to Batzulnéta's, and in the evening had a grand orgie.

At first we were told that it would require thirty days to cross the mountains, but, after many *wahwahs*, it was decided that with long marches the journey could be accomplished in seven. The first estimate was made on our arrival in a half exhausted condition.

Four natives were employed to pack across the mountains for us, but not until the Tyone had been first rewarded, then the fathers of the young men, and finally a promise from us to pay the young men themselves for their services.

The natives here differed not a great deal from those of Tarál. Their language, however, was not readily intelligible to our Lower River natives, one of whom I used as interpreter. In some cases their words were entirely different, for example: a long distance by the Midnóoskies was kuteshít; by the Tatlatans, nijót (French j).

Just before leaving a series of loud shouts was heard, proclaiming the first salmon of the season. It was a rather small silver salmon, which was placed in a conspicuous place on one of the spruce-bough tepees, where all visited it with great singing and glee. Though aware that probably in a few days there would be hundreds of these, the promise of honnái meat (caribou), at Lake Suslóta, induced us to move on. Moreover, I knew that at most only two or three days' rations of fresh fish could be carried.

The expedition left Batzulnéta's camp for Lake Suslóta, the source of a tributary of the Slaná River, on the 4th day of June. At three miles from camp the bearing of the pass over the mountains was N. 30° E., bearing of the source of the Copper River, E. 30° S. Almost the entire march to the lake was over a boggy flat, with *têtes de femmes*, or hummocks, a liberal allowance of scrub birch, so small that it might readily be taken for gooseberry bushes, and a limited quantity of dwarf spruce. About noon it was extremely difficult to find enough wood to boil the tea. The gravel and bowlder bed, so near the surface, would prevent the growth of vegetation of any considerable size, even though there were no ice.

The mountains we were soon to cross were comparatively low, and pointed almost at right angles to the high mountains to our eastward and southward. The high mountains in question constitute the apex of the mountain system south of the Yukon, and from which spurs shoot in several directions. The headwaters of the Tananá, Copper, and White Rivers, are contained in them. The location of the prominent peaks, viz, Sanford, Drum, Wrangell, Tillman, and Blackburn, by numerous compass bearings, do not tend to show the continuity of the range. Could a view have been obtained from one of these peaks, a backbone of the system might have been determined, showing the connection with the St. Elias Range, with the mountains that separate the Copper from the Tananá, and those between the Tananá and the White. The existence of high mountains behind and around Tarál, and the high mountains north of Prince William's Sound led me to believe that the St. Elias Range finds an extension at a rather uniform distance from the coast, and terminates south of the Kuskokwim. The mountains we were about to cross could hardly be a continuation of the high mountains to the east, unless one be considered a spur of the other. The range, south of the middle part of the Tananá, contains some very high, snow-clad peaks.

We reached Lake Suslóta, at the foot of the pass, where we found one house and three or four families, consisting of eight men, six women, and nine children. Their main sustenance was a dried fish, much smaller in size than the salmon. They were not fishing during our stay. In the lake, which was only two miles long and very narrow, could be seen small grayling, but they could not be induced to rise for anything we could offer them, no insects of any description being obtainable. From Suslóta, Mount Sanford had a bearing of SSW. and an angle of elevation of 4° 2′. It towered above all visible surroundings. The outlet of the lake, a tributary of the Slaná, flowed in a southwesterly direction.

For many days before reaching Lake Suslóta we had sought a pass through the mountains on the right bank, which continued to grow lower as our northings increased. To be at the foot of such a one as would lead to the Tananá in so short a time seemed hardly credible, but such was the fact. To find two rivers of the magnitude of the Tananá and Copper heading so near each other as almost to have intersecting tributaries, and to be so entirely different in their characteristics, I consider one of the most interesting discoveries of the expedition.   The barometer showed Camp Suslóta to be 3,160 feet above the sea-level.   The narrative of the Copper River ends with Suslóta, the journey over the mountains being included in the narrative of the Tananá River.

NARRATIVE OF THE TANANÁ RIVER.

LAKE SUSLÓTA TO TETLING'S.

I begin the narrative of the Tananá at the initial point of the pass over the Alaskan Range, Lake Suslóta. This pass I have named in honor of General N. A. Miles, U. S. Army. It is probably the best locality that will permit communication beteen the Yukon Basin and the Copper River country, and would doubtless be used should the minerals of the latter region prove of sufficient importance to justify such expenditures as this would necessitate. The possibility of the ascent of the Copper with provisions can hardly be entertained, unless it be made with sleds during the winter.

The route (Miles's Pass) from the headwaters of the Copper to the Upper Tananá, and the finding on both sides of natives who had been to the Yukon River to trade, settles the mooted question, "Do the Copper River natives visit the Yukon?" With regard to this matter the traders themselves were not confident, until a few questions were put, which brought forth the facts in the matter. Mr. McQuisten, trader of Fort Reliance, and Mr. La Due, a prospector, asserted that they had seen some Copper River natives at the post in 1883, and that a native on the north side of the mountains was used as a second interpreter to them. From this and other information I conclude that their visits are not frequent, and that traffic is effected usually by intermediate parties.

About noon of June 5, 1885, after engaging natives, taking observations for position and arranging the packs of all, including those of the dogs, we left the settlement, and soon began the ascent of the mountains, which were free from snow excepting the highest points and the ravines. The upper or northerly end of Lake Suslóta was yet covered with ice and snow. As we slowly ascended the rather gradual slope, the Copper River basin appeared before our eyes, a beautiful sight. Looking south the lofty mountains on the east bank, the flat country on the west, with numerous small lakes, hedged in with evergreen timber; the river itself, with numerous channels, made an impression long to be retained. On our left, while ascending, was visible the small tributary emptying into Suslóta. Up it is a trail used by the natives in going to Lake Mentásta, the source of Slaná River.

After having reached an elevation of 1,000 feet above Suslóta, in traveling about 3 miles, we found in our front a continuation of mountains, the highest of which was 1,000 feet above us, but which looked insignificant when compared with the lofty white masses to our south and east. From this elevation was pointed out to us by the natives the direction of Lake Mentásta, which was nearly due north; also a prominent pyramidal peak, towards which our course lay, and which bore NNE.

After a march of about 7 miles we were near the foot of Mount "Tebay," pyramidal in shape and on a brook which feeds Lake Suslóta. To our great surprise and delight the long-looked for salmon were endeavoring to ascend it. In some of the little channels the ice prevented further progress, in other places there was so little water that the fish, in endeavoring to push their way up on their sides, actually shoved themselves out of the brook onto the land. These were the advance guard that had doubtless passed through Suslóta after our start in the morning. We had no difficulty in taking all we needed, nor was there any hesitancy about one and all eating until completely satisfied—a most unusual occurrence.

We had about three days' supply of meat on hand, which was about all we could carry, under the circumstances. I know this seems rather incredible, but not more so than the fact that any one of the party could easily eat 4 pounds of meat at a sitting. One of the party ate three salmon, including the heads of all and the roe of one from the time of going into camp until retiring. This camp (No. 1) was the only place between Núchek and the Yukon River where it would have been possible to lie over and obtain food in sufficient quantity to satisfy our hunger; yet I did not deem it prudent to attempt to recuperate our strength on fish diet alone.

With one day's ration of salmon, and our moose meat, we left camp No. 1 and traveled NE. ½ N., 5 miles, passing the little lake to which the salmon were making in order to deposit their spawn. I asked our natives whether these fish ever descended. They replied in the negative, thus in a measure corroborating the same views held by some of the natives of the Yukon.

One and a half miles further brought us to a water-shed between the Tananá and Copper, where, for the first time, was sighted the long sought Tananá waters. At this place were many small lakes, separated by only a few hundred yards, some serving as reservoirs for the Tananá and others for the Copper. The natives informed me that Lake Mentásta had outlets flowing into both the Tananá and Copper. Should this not be strictly true, I am satisfied from the topography of the country that the headwaters of Tokái River are not more than a mile or two from the lake. This so-called watershed is in reality a pass, 800 to 1,500 feet lower than the mountains on each side, that are barren of everything save a little grass, spruce, and much moss. From it the course to Lake Mentásta is nearly due west.

On each side of us and converging as we advanced were two tributaries of Tokái River, one of which was reported to head in Lake Mentásta, the other headed to the east and south. It would have been the most natural course to have followed this tributary to the Tananá, but our packers protested, saying we would starve. Our general course for the day was NE., and our camp No. 2, below the junction of the two tributaries, was near the cañon through which the Tokái River flows, and on its left bank, at a distance of 10 miles from camp. Then instead of following this stream to its confluence with the Tananá we crossed it a few miles below camp, and a mile or two farther on a tributary of it; then began ascending to another height, from which Tokái River bore NNW. At 8.30 p. m. our course had now become due east, with another tributary of Tokái River on our left, flowing nearly due west. At 10.45 p. m. we went into Camp 3, on the second water-shed, where were numerous small lakes, and other geographical features similar to those on the first. The term water-shed must here be considered in a limited sense, inasmuch as the entire range would properly receive that term; and it must also be remembered that our course was nearer east than north. Observation, on the 7th, showed our latitude to be 63.11; on the 5th, at Suslóta, 63.01.

Fatigue and heat prevented a start from Camp 3 until 5 p. m., at which time the sun was far above the horizon. The course for 4 miles was east; then was begun the ascent of a tributary of a stream emptying into the Tananá to the east of the place where we first reached that river. The bearing for the next few miles was NE., until we reached a second tributary of the stream on our right, just mentioned. From this the course was ENE., up a gorge, with much snow and ice, and temperature below freezing point.

At 1.30 a. m., after the steepest ascent made by the expedition, we were on a very short and narrow "divide," 4,500 feet above the sea-level, with bold, barren bluffs on each side. From this the most grateful sight it has ever been my fortune to witness was presented. The sun was rising, but not in the east, in fact just two points east of north. We had nearly reached the "land of the midnight sun," to find in our front the "promised land." The views in advance and in rear were both grand; the former showing the extensive Tananá Valley with numerous lakes, and the low unbroken range of mountains between the Tananá and Yukon Rivers. On this pass, with both white and yellow buttercups around me and snow within a few feet, I sat proud of the grand sight which no visitor save an Atnatána or Tananátana had ever seen. Fatigue and hunger were for the time forgotten in the great joy at finding our greatest obstacles overcome. As many as twenty lakes were visible, some of which were north of

the Tananá, more than 20 miles away. The bearing of the most
easterly water was E. 15° N. The bearing to Nandell's, our immediate destination, was E. 30° N. Had we ascended the craggy,
rocky peak on our right, which obstructed the eastern view, we could
probably have traced the Tananá many miles towards its source,
but the greatest of all obstacles to exploration, hunger, prevented.
The northern declivity was extremely abrupt, and our descent lay
along a gorge similar to the one ascended, excepting the absence of
ice and snow. A mile down this gorge, at the first obtainable timber, we halted and cooked the last Liebig's extract of beef, that we
had so carefully preserved for just such a contingency.

At 5 a. m. we went into Camp 4, barely able to stand, to be har-
rassed by the gnats and mosquitoes. Our only protection was our
blankets, which the extreme heat rendered most uncomfortable. We
had succeeded by marching all night in making about 14 miles. We
had crossed the Alaskan Mountains, represented in this section on
all charts that attempt vertical delineations as very rugged and
lofty, which is hardly the case. Not four weeks before our landing
at San Francisco, a scout sent into Alaska the year preceding us
had returned and reported that a crossing from the Copper to the
Tananá would be utterly impossible; that a fair idea of the nature
of the country could be obtained by placing one Mount Hood on
another. His information was obtained from natives, and is not
more inaccurate than is frequently obtained from the same source.
The traders of the Yukon, who are supposed to be more familiar with
the general topography of the interior than any other white men,
believed the crossing to be next to impossible, and were more than
surprised when we reached the Yukon River.

Camp 4, just over the range, was at an elevation of 3,300 feet, as
shown by the barometer.

June 9 we began our tramp about 2 p. m., and having been informed by the natives that by marching all night we could reach
Nandell's, we decided upon making an attempt to do so, provided we
had no success at hunting. Two natives, sent in advance to shoot
rabbits, were overtaken at 10 p. m. with one in their possession. This
little animal was but a scanty exasperating taste for nine half-starved
men. During the remainder of the march to Nandell's, so exhausted
was the party that the slowest progress was barely possible.

Just before sighting the few houses at the settlement, we were on
a hill two or three hundred feet above the lakes and could see that
the chain to which they belong is very extensive. We had passed
several small lakes, and had crossed a large brook, leaving it on our
left. This last may have been a feeder of some of the lakes, but from
its temperature I should judge that such is not the case. The general
course was E. 30° N., with many deviations.

At 3 a. m., June 10, the party was welcomed at Nandell's with a great firing of guns. Here there were forty men, twenty-eight women, and eighteen children assembled to gaze at a sight never before seen. Many of the men of this locality, in fact most of them, had made the tour one or more times to the Yukon for trading purposes, yet some of the men and most of the women and children had never seen a white man. Their clothing indicated more easy communication with a trading station than did that of the Atnatánas. We realized from their appearance that better times awaited us.

A few of the boys, to their great pride and our surprise, repeated, with various degrees of accuracy, the letters of the alphabet. They had received instruction on the Yukon from Mr. Simms, the zealous missionary sent out from England. He was highly esteemed by the natives, who were much benefited by his worthy example and instruction. This most excellent gentleman passed his last moments on Porcupine or Rat River, in the year 1884.

Had the distance to Nandell's been 30 miles farther, and game equally scarce as on the trail traveled, the injury to the party from hunger would have been incalculable.

The settlement of which Nandell was autocrat consisted of four houses situated on a small, clear stream, which helped connect the chain of lakes. After crossing the mountains a most decided change of landscape was presented us. Vegetation was more rank, and the temperature of the lake water was so high as to make it very disagreeable to drink. It seemed rather remarkable that the season should be far enough advanced (June 10) for the sun's heat to have caused the water to be not uncomfortable for bathing in these lakes. The water of the Yukon was very much colder in July, as was the water of the Tananá the last of June. In fact, the mouths of some of the tributaries of the Tananá were filled with ice as we passed them. Some of the lakes seemed to possess a great depth of water, though a more thorough investigation might have revealed otherwise. Possibly only the shallow and surface water is heated by the sun, which shines in that latitude, in June, about twenty-one hours per day. The psychrometer was stolen before the temperature of the water had been obtained, and our barometer was so injured as to be of no future use to us. These incidents came near being the cause of serious trouble. I knew well enough that the manifestation of any fear would place us completely in the power of the natives, to treat us as they should see fit. Efforts to recover the instrument, however, were of no avail, and we barely averted a struggle with these people.

The country in the vicinity of the lakes was covered with a luxuriant growth of grass, and countless roses were in bloom. The trails round about bore evidence of having been much used, and altogether a more civilized appearance had not been seen since leaving Nuchek. The houses were large, and constructed without the use of bark.

The absence of the attached sweat-room and of the "box" arrangement of the interior caused a marked difference in their appearance
when compared with the typical Copper River house.   To procure
firewood even for cooking was not an easy task.   The scarcity of
timber showod that these grounds had been used many years.   A
very old native informed me that he had boon born there; that during the winter wood was hauled on sleds from the hills; that Nandell had obtained his supremacy by plunging a knife into his rival,
son of my informant; that there were no salmon in the Tananá.

I learned that there was a trail from Lake Mentásta to Nandell's, and also to the Tananá; that there were two routes to Fort
Reliance—one entirely by foot, the other by portage to a tributary
of the White River, then down the same, the White and the Yukon,
in a skin boat.   The return trip was always by the former route.

The food of the natives at this season is chiefly fish, taken in this
stream by means of a dip-net which just fills the channel, made narrow by means of small spruce piles driven side by side.   Here there
were several kinds of them, including pickerel, suckers, grayling,
and two varieties of whitefish.   The "catch" in the single dip-net
supplied all, and from each fisherman Nandell exacted a *royalty*.
Some one was on the fishing-stand with net in hand day and night.
At Nandell's was obtained the first *pemmican* that we had seen in
the territory.   Afterwards, however, some was obtained on a tributary of the Kóyukuk.

The inhabitants around these lakes, including Tetling's following,
were almost without exception suffering from severe coughs, and
many showed unmistakable signs of pulmonary troubles.

From Nandell's, Lake Mentásta bore nearly due west.   The canoes
used here and at Kheeltat's are the smallest I have ever known, an
average one being 13 to 15 feet long, 21 to 24 inches of beam, and 11
to 12 inches across the bottom, and very shallow.

At first a raft journey down the Tananá was contemplated, but the
natives protested, saying that two *moons* would be required.   Later
developments showed conclusively that a raft would have been totally unfit to run rapids so strewn with timber in places that we could
barely run our skin boat through.   It was finally decided by a coun-
cil that the Yukon (Niga To) could be reached in a skin boat in
twenty days, but no Indians could be induced to assist us farther
than to the next settlement, two days distant by the river from Tetling's.

Nandell's is in latitude 63° 21', and approximate longitude 143° 28'.
He had several "medicine men" in his following, one of whom accompanied us as far as Tetling's, entreating us not to stop at Kheeltat's, saying that all of us would certainly be killed.

June 12 we left Nandell's for Tetling's, which bore NNE., and
which is about 11 miles distant.   The destruction of the natural

carpeting of the earth by fire to kill the mosquitoes and gnats has caused a splendid growth of grass between the two points just named. The numerous lakes on each side of the trail, the meadow-like appearance of parts of the land between, with groves of cottonwood interspersed with birch, was sufficient to recall scenes of much lower latitudes. Around these lakes the country seemed more pastoral in its nature than in any part of the Territory. A yet more pleasing fact was that there were few mosquitoes or gnats to harrass us.

TETLING'S TO KHEELTAT'S.

We reached Tetling's in the afternoon, and had the construction of the baidárra immediately begun — that is, if the word "immediately" can ever be properly used with regard to fulfillment of agreements by these people. Only three caribou skins could be obtained for it, one each from Nandell and Tetling, and one from quite a distance. At Tetling's were six men who had greeted us at Nandell's, four women, and seven children, occupying two houses situated on a deep, clear stream, the outlet of a lake much larger than any we had passed — so said the natives. To obtain the positions of the lakes in the vicinity would have required a much more accurate survey than it was possible for us to make.

Had there been food, I should have sent three of the party over the portage to the Yukon, and would have gone with the others to the source of the Tananá, which is indicated on the general chart in dotted lines. Insufficiency of food here as elsewhere was our greatest source of anxiety. The exhausted condition of the party caused me to start down the Tananá as soon as possible, vainly hoping that on reaching the Yukon our wants would be immediately supplied. We purchased all obtainable food at Nandell's and Tetling's, giving in exchange all the money that remained and every garment or article of any description that could be spared. The men of the party volunteered to give up everything in their possession, even to coats, shirts, pocket-knives, &c. We paid dearly for every pound of food, yet we left the natives in a hungry state, with their sole dependence on fish, which at that season were not abundant. The absence of salmon in the Tananá caused me to suspect falls or severe rapids in the river, but these natives denied that such was the case, though flatly refusing to go to the Yukon with us, notwithstanding the greatest inducements.

At this place I noticed that the severe hardships to which Bremner had so long been exposed were affecting both his mental and physical constitution. His ankle, sprained on the Chittystone, had assumed an unusual size, which was due, as we found later, to scurvy. For two weeks past the body of Sergeant Robertson had been covered with black spots, which developed later into another form of scurvy. We had carried a bottle of acetic acid, the best anti-scor-butic that could be obtained in Sitka and that could be transported. Its use was not effective, and I doubt whether any other acid would have been.

The baidárra having been completed, was launched by the native boys, given a trial trip, and found satisfactory. It did not differ materially from the one we had constructed and used on the Copper River. Instead of being constructed out of moose skins, those of the caribou were used, and it was by no means an easy task to secure even three in all that region.

With two natives, our three pack-dogs, and a large supply of meat and fish we started down the stream at 6 a. m. on the 14th. There were six paddlers and one steersman. After a run of two and a half hours down Tetling River, with its many windings and general course of N. by E., we reached the muddy Tananá, with its quick-sands and boilings, sand-spits, and absence of rocks. The current of the river was between 3 and 3½ miles per hour. Its water was covered with foam, which was not necessarily attributable to falls, new foam having been passed several times en route down. Spruce grew down to the very banks of the river. No attempt will be made in this narrative to detail the numerous courses; suffice it to say that the exact time on each course, as well as the course itself, were recorded, and the reduced results are shown on the accompanying maps. At 6 p. m. rocky banks on the north side were seen for the first time. The actual run on the Tananá was a distance of 35 miles.

Heavy smoke caused by the extensive timber fires obscured the sun the entire day, so that an observation was impossible. This smoke had originated from signal fires which were intended to give warning of our presence in the country. When we first arrived at Nandell's there was only an occasional smoke around, but as his guests departed for their different habitations each marked his trail by a signal fire. The prevailing wind was from the east and carried the smoke along with us. In answer to the fires on the south bank new ones were started on the north, so that for nearly two days we barely caught a glimpse of the sun except through the heavy spruce smoke.

Camp No. 7 was left at 5.45 a. m. to follow the many windings of the Tananá, which now varied from 100 to 300 yards in width. Most of the spruce timber growing along its banks was from 3 to 8 inches in diameter. At 8 o'clock the mouth of Tokái River, which had much increased in size since our first sight of it, was passed on the left bank. It does not possess the torrent current of other tributaries farther down on the same side. In the forenoon the first gravel banks were seen. The mountains on the left bank were becoming closer to the river, and the "country rock" had become visible on both banks. Nearly all the islands in this part of the river are timber covered.

19.—NABESNATÁNAS—KHEELTAT, HIS SON, AND DESHADDY.

The signal smoke of Kheeltat, the bushy-headed Tyone, was sighted early in the middle of the afternoon, and at 6.30 we halted at some of his cache houses opposite the point on the left bank where the trail from Lake Mentasta reaches the Tananá. At this place, in accordance with my promise, I permitted the two natives to return to Nandell, which they intended to do by walking across the country. After a run down the river of 4 miles we halted for the night on the north bank, and about one-half mile above a tributary 30 yards wide with muddy water similar to the Tananá. During the day we had traveled on forty-one different courses, and the actual time (exclusive of halts) consumed was eleven hours and a half, the distance 45 miles.

After we had been in camp about an hour we heard the firing of guns, to which we responded. Shortly afterwards three natives appeared in camp. They were runners from Kheeltat, whose house they said was "kootel-stée," a short distance. This was the place that Nandell, Tetling, and their "medicine men" had so frequently implored me not to visit, but to silently pass by. Unwilling to pass through the country without knowing the disposition of the natives, and realizing that the danger incurred by the visit was scarcely greater than those we were accustomed to meet and would probably in the future encounter, I resolved to see the warlike Tyone. The traders of the Yukon informed us in July that they supposed Kheeltat would be hostile to any whites invading his territory. The runners had descended Kheeltat River in two small canoes, which they said could be utilized by us. At 11 p. m. Fickett and myself started for Kheeltat's, having been carried to the right bank of the tributary in the canoes, and having the youngest of the three natives for a guide. At 1.30 a. m., June 16, after a forced march over country showing no signs of a trail, we walked into the miserable looking house of Kheeltat, very much fatigued. The accompanying picture represents Kheeltat, the bushy-haired Tyone, his son, and a sub-Tyone, Deshaddy, who had preceded us from Nandell's to give information of our arrival.

It was taken when they were on a trading expedition to the Yukon, and consequently dressed in their finest. With less decoration and less modern clothes upon the persons it would be a fair picture of the Upper Tananá men. As we entered, a frown spread over Kheeltat's face and he would say nothing. The absence of the customary salute to welcome us was rather ominous, and his silence was yet more so.

Shortly after our arrival a few shots were fired, not in honor of us, but to assemble the clans; couriers were also dispatched for the same purpose.

Exhausted by working since 5 in the morning, Fickett and myself immediately fell asleep, to find on our awaking two hours later, twenty-six men and four squaws in the small house, all attired in their best. The chart was shown them and the object of my visit explained, all of which interested them but little. My reputation as a "medicine man" had preceded me, and when I produced my medicines, consisting of three kinds of pills, viz, quinine, and the usual Army purgative and anti-purgative pills, I immediately commanded their attention. Nandell had informed me that there had been many deaths among these people, and as nearly as I could understand him he feared they might attribute them to our entrance into the country, and this may have been one of the causes of his warnings to us.

The same warm lakes, the same general appearance here as at Nandell's characterized the country. The consumptive look and its accompanying cough were more marked here than at the former place, and doubtless cod-liver oil would have been a more suitable prescription than anything in my medicine chest. The pills were given indiscriminately, but seemed to satisfy the natives. I must correct this; there was some discrimination, for the chief received one of each kind, a minor chief one each of two kinds, and a man or woman a single pill.

Efforts to get two natives to go a part or all of the way to the Yukon were of no avail. From them we learned that there were remarkable features in the Tananá River, either violent rapids or falls. They would point to the canoes, make gestures indicative of capsizing, at the same time spreading the fingers of the hand and imitating with the voice the roaring sound of the water. From Kheeltat's there is a portage over to the Yukon at Fetútlin—the station now occupied by Mr. Harper, which requires six days, one of which is by water. The bushy-haired chief and all his following went to the mouth of the stream (Kheeltat's River) with us, the former taking me in the canoe with him. Like all the natives we had thus far met, they insisted on selling us their few furs, and seemed surprised that we were not traders. On parting with this reputed warlike chief, he promised to meet me on the upper Yukon in July, when the steamboat would have arrived, and said he would carry me a piece of caribou. My plans were afterwards changed, and I have not since seen him.

KHEELTAT'S TO NUKLUKYET.

At 7.20 a. m. we started again down the Tananá, much to the displeasure of the natives, who insisted on making an examination of our effects which they could vaguely see in our skin boat. We now counted twenty-eight men, eighteen women, and six children, probably nearly all of Kheeltat's following.

At 4 miles below we passed the mouth of a small, clear stream on the left bank, and 8 below we were at the foot of very lofty yellow granite bluffs, in a state of rapid disintegration. From these "Cathe-

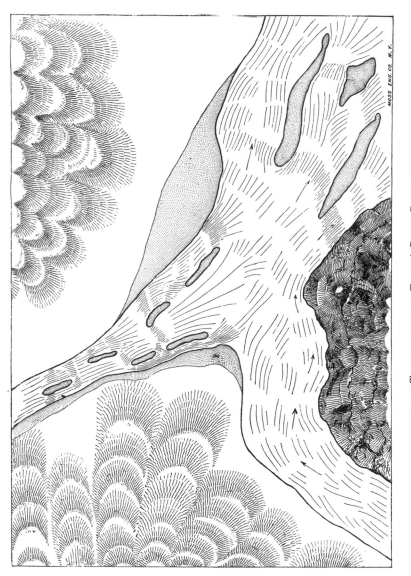

20.—Typical head of Tananá River Rapids.

dral Bluffs" the course for several miles was directly toward the mountains on the south bank. When at the very foot of the mountains the rushing of waters verified the statement of the natives, and we were indeed in rapids, whose course was nearly due west. For one half hour we were running them, wondering every minute what a few rods farther would reveal. The high waves in places indicated the presence of large rocks in the channel. These rapids (Cathedral Rapids) mark the place where the river cuts through a small range of mountains. Below them the land on each side is lower and the course of the river is much more to the northward. The hills on the right bank strongly resemble those on the Hudson in the vicinity of Newburg.

Ten miles below the head of Cathedral Rapids appeared yet more majestic bluffs (Tower Bluffs) on the right, with a torrent stream on the left, whose delta mouth was imbedded in a field of thick ice and snow. We were at the head of Tower Bluff Rapids. Ever afterwards the *torrent stream on the left with bluffs on the right was a sure index of very ragid water.*

The ice at the mouth of the tributary, called by me Robertson River,* was the first ice seen on the Tananá side of the mountains. The gulch from which Robertson River flows bears ·W. 20° S., and marks a decided break in the mountains to the westward. It also indicates the general course of the minor range, a cross-section of which is included between the head of Cathedral Rapids and the head ot Tower Bluff Rapids, through which the river had cut.

Just below Robertson River the Tananá spread its muddy water in several channels, which in turn are divided until in places we had a striking picture of Copper River.

After running in these rapids for 8 miles the current slackened to 6 miles per hour for a mile or two, when we were again in rapids not surpassed by those just run. The upper part of the rapids caused me to consider steamboat navigation doubtful, but with respect to those 15 miles below there could be no doubt. The river was so divided into channels that it was with difficulty we could keep our small craft from running aground on the pebbly bottom. We were occasionally aground, when probably to our right or left, within a few hundred feet, was deep water. Once in a channel there was no halting unless run aground.

In places the river-bed attained a width of a mile to a mile and a quarter, and contained fields of lodged timber with roots turned to the current. Some of this timber gave evidence of having but recently been washed away from the place of its growth, the roots filled in with soil still fresh. Other of it, having been barked, and having lost the small boughs, showed that it was lodged prior to the

---

* After a member of the party of same name.

breaking of the ice. Still other, from its well-seasoned appearance, showed that it had been lodged many years. These trees are known to Alaskan pioneers as sweepers, as are those which have the roots fast to the banks, with the trunks and boughs in the water. Besides these were huge piles of drift timber lodged in the gravel islands. The lodging of trees is continually creating new islands and hence new channels ; the river is constantly and rapidly cutting away banks, and new ones are being formed. High banks were seen which are so recent as to be covered with a growth of very small shrubbery only, while several feet below the surface may be seen the roots and trunks of larger trees, evidently not *in situ.* At the present time the wearing of the left bank seems to far exceed that of the right, as evidenced by the distance of the river in several places from bluffs on the north side, at the foot of which it rather recently flowed, and by the new channels through the timbered soil on the south side.

At 5 p. m. a halt was made for an observation for longitude and to measure the current. The latter, though decidedly less rapid than in many places during the day, was 6 miles per hour. We went into camp at 8 p. m., just below a small tributary on the north side, having worked ten hours in the boat, most of which was in rapids. The mountains on the left were showing themselves farther from the river and much higher.

Camp 9 was left at 6 a. m. to follow the river, now more nearly confined to a single channel. Just below camp were high bluffs on the right and a small stream on the left. Ten miles below camp the river and mountains on the south bank, with high rocky bluffs on the north side, were undoubted indications that other rapids were at hand.

I was loath to believe that the Tananá would not be a navigable river, but Tower Bluff Rapids emphatically settles the question, as do Carlisle Rapids, which begin with Johnson River.* This latter stream is in all respects similar to Robertson River, and also marks a decided break in the mountains on the south bank. The high bluffs on the right bank are contemporaneous with those farther up. Several compass observations gave a position for Mount Kimball, a prominent snow-covered peak, but not so lofty as the peaks farther to the west and south, seen later. Johnson River is very swift, with abundance of ice in its wide bed, and is nearly as large as Robertson River, whose volume probably does not exceed 30 by 3 feet.

After nine hours in the boat, during nearly all of which time we were in rapids, we went into Camp No. 10, well tired by the exertions made in avoiding shoals, stringers, and drift piles. For an hour during the afternoon so dangerous were the rapids that the steering paddle could not be dropped even sufficiently long to permit a compass observation.

---

* Named after a member of the party.

In order to get a noon observation for latitude, we did not leave Camp 10, June 18, until 1 p. m., when we began "shooting" channels filled in with timber so recently from the banks that the sod around the roots was in many places undisturbed. Eight miles farther down were hundreds of trees lodged in the channels and along the banks.

About 15 miles below Camp 10 a swift and muddy stream in a single channel empties from the south. This tributary of the Tananá I have called Gerstle River.* It is about fifty feet wide and seems very deep. It marks the end of the rapids, below which the current is about 4 to 5 miles per hour.

Four miles below Gerstle River, Goodpaster River, one of the largest tributaries, empties from the north, is 25 yards wide, and has a very swift current, with water similar to the Tananá. At its junction was a deserted fishing station and canoes, the only sign of natives seen since leaving Kheeltat's. This river was described by Kheeltat as having houses on it, and large fish in it, which I presume meant salmon. It is probably the limit of the salmon run. It is not strange that there are no inhabitants along that part of the river just described; such a current would forbid any sort of navigation and would make an undesirable home for even a Tananatána.

The smallness of the tributaries of the Tananá is one of its special characteristics. Five miles below this tributary the land near the river on both sides is flat, with a very limited quantity of timber, most of which is dwarf birch. The banks are covered with moss and grass. The lowness of the country caused us to suspect that the Yukon was near, but we were mistaken then and several times later. The only game we had thus far seen on the river, besides one porcupine and one gray wolf, was an occasional lynx or rabbit, more seldom a pair of geese.

Camp 11 was made in a rain storm, to secure protection against which we sought the densest cottonwood timber, which by this time we had learned to fell and so place as to give the greatest protection. Sometimes, however, the greater part of the night was passed in a pool of water, efforts to better our situation being of no avail. With the exception of a few days on the Chittystone River, we had worn our clothes day and night since March 20. That this, as well as the scanty quantity and unusual quality of food, together with the exposure, assisted in sowing the seeds of scurvy there can be no doubt.

On the morning of June 19 we left Camp 11 after having made the accompanying sketch of the high mountains to the south. Five miles below, a small stream on the left, with a single vacated house at its mouth, was passed. Just below it is the only place where the

---

*Having no natives with us and finding none along this part of the Tananá, we were unable to assign native names to the tributaries.

S.   S. 9 W

SW. by S.   Ang. el. 2⁰ 40′   SW. ½ S.

21.—Sketch of mountains south of Tananá River

NT NINE MILES ABOVE THE MOUTH OF VOLKMAR RIVER.

river attains as small a width as 80 yards, yet the current at this place (Mason's Narrows) is not more than 5 miles per hour.

Four miles below Mason's Narrows, Volkmar River, the first tributary in size, empties on the north side. This, too, was a muddy stream, with a rather sluggish current. It was also described to us by Kheeltat as a fish stream. There were no signs of habitation at its junction save the ashes of a camp fire ; though 4 miles below, on the opposite bank, were three houses, one of which was probably used as a winter home. All were unoccupied. Here were graves covered with cotton cloth ; the first monuments of this type we had seen. This method of marking the graves is very common on the Yukon.

Four miles below Goodpaster River is a mountain torrent on the left bank, high cliffs on the right, and the head of Bates Rapids. As soon as we arrived opposite the bluffs the swiftness of the current was recognized. The river, which just above is in a single channel, spreads until in places it is $1\frac{1}{2}$ miles wide. Fifteen to twenty miles below the head of these rapids there are so many channels that we with difficulty found sufficient water to float our skin boat. The current all day, with the exception of a few miles above these rapids, had an average rate of $5\frac{1}{2}$ to 6 miles per hour. At 6 p. m. we went into Camp 12, having paddled ten and a quarter hours.

Two miles below camp on the left bank a small torrent washes through the timbered woods. It possesses a delta mouth to an exaggerated degree, all filled in with spruce timber. A few hundred yards below it were seen in tents the only natives since leaving Kheeltat's. There were two women and one girl in the party, the men of it being absent for food. These were also the first natives who spoke of the river by the name Tananá. Above this part it is known as Nabesná River. Their fishing stand was erected and dip-net at hand, but the salmon had not yet arrived; hence a hungry appearance prevailed. Half a mile below there were two fair-looking but unoccupied houses.

During the afternoon of the 20th, below Camp 12, large masses of driftwood and sunken soil, with its vegetation partly submerged, were passed; yet further down the river seemed to have no bounds, having attained a width, as best we could estimate, of from 3 to 4 miles. After nine and a quarter hours of paddling Camp 13 was made.

This was left at 3 a. m. the following morning, June 21. Twenty miles below camp the current is more nearly confined to a single channel and is very much less rapid. On the last part of the run the current was about 3 to $3\frac{1}{2}$ miles per hour. Two small streams (one on each side, as shown on the map) were passed during the day, as well as several fishing stations, none of which were occupied. Our rations of meat and fish had been consumed, and we were living entirely on the fat and tallow that had been reserved to fry fresh fish in, should it be obtained. After thirteen and a half hours on the water we made camp below the largest house seen on the Tananá, but which had, from its appearance, not been used for several seasons. There were two flag-poles and several large birch canoes lying near. It is possible that these people, like the Midnoóskies, burn or desert the house upon the death of its master. I know no other assignable cause why this house should not have been occupied the previous season.

One mile below Camp 14 a small stream was passed on the left; 10 miles below and on the same side, a somewhat larger stream of clear water. Living on tallow only, without any chance of obtaining even rabbits, was not conducive to cheerfulness of mind, though we were running down stream. After eight hours on the water we were surprised to find two small tents on the north bank. All hands paddled with renewed energy towards them, to the consternation of the occupants, who, with guns in hands, rushed to the brush. An old man, a woman, and two children remained. From them we obtained forty-two small white dried fish, to be served with the tallow or grease. The weather had become very warm for a few hours during the middle of the days and our diet correspondingly disagreeable. The current of the river during the day varied from 3 to 5 miles and was generally confined to a single channel.

At 9 p. m., having paddled fourteen hours, we halted on a sand-spit in the middle of the river to avoid the mosquitoes, which had now become a great pest. The distance traveled could scarcely be less than 55 miles. During the day several unoccupied fishing stations were passed. The absence of the mountains on the left was marked.

From Camp 15 to the mouth of the Toclat River the current varies from $3\frac{1}{2}$ to 4 miles per hour, and the river is confined to a single channel, excepting where an occasional wooded island divides it. No mountains are visible on either side. During the run of the 23d (twelve hours) no sign of a house was seen, nor was there any on the 24th until the Toclat River was reached.

This river is about 20 to 25 yards wide at its mouth, and is partly the means of communication between the natives of the lower Tananá and the upper Kuskokwim, the second river in size in Alaska. Toclat in the native tongue means *dishwater*. On its right bank are two summer-houses, and on its left nine, an excellent proof that it is a good river for fishing purposes. It may be well to state here that if the exploration of the upper waters of the Kuskokwim is contemplated, the portage from the Toclat would be the most feasible route. The lower waters of the Kuskokwin were explored by the Russians many years ago, and more recently by Messrs. Petroff and Williams, but its upper waters are yet unknown to white man. The

Toclat flows along the foot of a minor range of mountains on its left bank, whose bearing is NE. and SW.

Two miles below it a camp of natives *en route* up the Tananá was reached. These had on hand a little meat and plenty of fresh king salmon, the first of the season. Our condition had already become serious, and had we not obtained food when we did from these natives we would have been in a most sad state on reaching the Yukon. Had we started down the Tananá two weeks earlier the probabilities are that we would not have seen a single native on the river. It must be remembered that Nandell's, Tetling's, and Kheeltat's people live on small streams away from the river, as do probably all the inhabitants during the springtime.

The camp of natives we had just passed was the following of Ivan, the most influential Tyone of the lower Tananá.

Their appearance in camp, at the very edge of the water, with thirty-five to forty birch canoes of all sizes fastened to the shore, the abundance of the rich-colored king salmon, split and hung up over the water, out of reach of the numerous dogs that had gone hungry most of the winter, was picturesque in the extreme. Their surroundings were luxurious when compared to ours. It seemed that we had never seen bedding look so clean and comfortable, or the colors of calico so fresh. They were indeed cleanly when compared to us. We felt sure that we must be near the place whence their merchandise had come, and where plenty awaited us. Ivan's following consisted of thirty-five men, twenty women, and twenty children.

About 20 miles below Toclat River is the log house once used by Mr. Harper as a trading station also the scene of Mrs. Bean's murder while her husband was a fur trader there.

Several miles above, the river follows along the foot of slaty bluffs, which show the last range through which the Tananá cuts. After passing them it becomes very wide and sluggish, with sometimes several channels. The volume of water is very great, as proved by the 20-foot sounding above Toclat River, where the river is 1,000 yards. The run of the 24th was ten hours in a current not greater than $3\frac{1}{2}$ miles per hour.

On the 25th we left the last camp on the Tananá, and after eight and one-half hours on the water were at the Yukon, a fact we did not recognize until informed by a woman, who halted us 2 miles below the junction by firing a gun.

We had supposed there was a place called Nuklúkyet (Nuklukáhyet, Nuclucayette), as shown on the most recent map, at the junction of the Yukon and Tananá. It is merely the ground where the natives formerly assembled for trading purposes. Where we halted were two women and three children, who informed us that Nukilerai was below, Nuklúhyet above. Nukilerái is the name by which the natives know the trading station. Having obtained a canoe, Pete and my-

22.—IVAN, A NUKLUKTÁNA TYONE.

24.—Nuklukyet—a winter picture.

MOSS ENG CO N Y.

23.—Nuklúkvet—A Summer Picture.

self, with one of the women as guide, went back to the junction to find not even a fishing station. Furthermore, the woman, in her Russo-Yukon dialect, informed us, much to our chagrin, that "Nukilerai, Kooshat natoo, chai natoo," which meant that there was no food or tea at the trading station below. It was too true. We immediately set out for this place, which will in the future be called Nuklúkyet, in accordance with the name now applied to it by the traders of the river.

We arrived at 2.30 a. m., where we received a cordial welcome from the half-breed, Andrew (Androosky), left in charge. The subsistence stores at the station consisted of about 3 dozen hard crackers, 3 quarts of beans, 20 pounds of flour, a little salt, and some machine oil. The steamboats *Yukon*, owned by the Alaska Commercial Company, and *New Racket*, owned by Messrs. Harper, McQuisten Mayo, traders, were vainly expected up the river from Saint Michael's in ten or twelve days; during their absence we must live on fish fried in machine oil.

Fortunately, the morning of our arrival two miners, who had wintered on the Yukon, Messrs. La Due and Franklin, arrived from the Upper Yukon with about 75 pounds of flour, 50 of which they kindly let us have. This lasted four days, though used very economically.

25.—Nowikákat in winter, showing dogs and sled.

NUKLÚKYET TO NULÁTO AND RETURN.

On arriving at Nuklúkyet steps were at once taken to rate our watch and to determine our position. A few days later the watch stopped on account of the butt of regulator having slipped off the hair spring and out of its normal position. This having been re-placed, rating was again attempted in spite of cloudy and rainy weather. On such expeditions at least three members of the party should be provided with pocket chronometers or best-grade watches.

While stopping at Nuklúkyet we depended on fish for nourishment until after the arrival of the steamboats. The run of the king salmon was almost ended. After them came the dog, then the silver, then the hump-back salmons, and with all a few whitefish. It must not be inferred from this that all of the kinds of salmon could not be taken on the same day, but that the advance guard of each arrive in the order named.

The natives from Tananá, Fort Yukon, and the Kóyukuk began to arrive by the last of June on their usual trading and pleasure ex-peditions. On July 4 the station was indeed thronged with natives, all of whom were disposed to be sociable and to help to share our small apartments. Once divested of its novelty their society was not to be envied. They indulged in jumping, wrestling, and a game of ball peculiar to themselves. To show their patriotism a grand firing of guns announced July 4, a flag was immediately run up the newly-made pole, and a general shouting and dancing indulged in. In their zeal they had begun their salute before midnight of July 3. At noon we fired a national salute ; and in the evening was a general dance, followed by special native dances. The arrival of an old man from the settlement a few miles above was the occasion of an ex-planation and apology from me for having broken into his caches. When told that hunger had been the cause and that a reparation would be made on the arrival of the steamboats, he replied that his people would do the same when hungry, and left satisfied.

Saturday, July 11, with Joseph La Due and the Tyone's son, I left Nuklúkyet to meet the steamboat, which was daily expected. That portion of the Yukon traveled during this canoe voyage has been run in with the compass observations taken by me, and differs but little from the same on the chart prepared by Captain Raymond, 1869. Our first camp was at the trading station, 2½ miles above the Nowi-kákat River and on the north bank. The agent, Mr. Cochrein, a

Russian, like all the traders of the river, was at Saint Michael's, or rather on the way up the river from that base of supplies. The picture represents the station in winter.

We had passed the Melozikákat River, the largest tributary entering from the north between the Tananá and Kóyukuk Rivers. La Due prospected on it for about 75 miles. It may be well to state here that I did not keep a record of all the islands passed on the river, as I did later on the Kóyukuk, because I assumed this had been previously done. The river has frequent wooded islands, but they are not so numerous that they could not be approximately located in such a running survey.

The Nowikákat, claimed by some to be 400 miles long, is the largest tributary of the Yukon, excepting the Tananá and White Rivers, entering it on the south side. There has been some mining claims located on it by Mr. Cochrein. It is a stream of considerable proportions and should be mapped, though, judging from the topography of the country, I do not think its length can exceed 250 miles. It would be navigable quite a distance with a small steam-launch. Native settlements are frequent along this portion of the river. We passed daily three to five, each of which contained twelve to twenty souls. From some of these we obtained a few berries or young ducks, or perhaps a handful of flour, all of which, with the activity necessitated by traveling, probably saved me from the scurvy and other sickness, with which the party was suffering at Nuklúkyet. For the food obtained along the route I could only promise payment on the arrival of the steamboat, which we were continually looking forward to. The farther we descended the river the more fish we found, but in other respects the more poverty-stricken the natives. This is explained by the scarcity of game, consequently the fewness of skins with which to clothe themselves and to barter for white man's clothing materials and household conveniences.

On the night of July 14 we landed at Nuláto, after a run of 201 miles. There are three Nulátos, viz: Lower, Middle, and Upper. The former was used as a station during the Russian rule, but after having been burned, Upper Nulato, where we stopped, was chosen and used until abandoned this year. The middle settlement is on the small stream which empties half a mile above the lower village and one mile below the upper. It was the post of the so-called "opposition company," and used by that corporation until its retirement from the country. Nearly all the natives of Yukon, certainly all that can afford it, use tents during the summer time. They possess the advantage of portabilty and are more effective than the summer houses in keeping out mosquitoes. I have, however, occasionally seen mosquito bars swung in a tent.

The delay at Nuláto was very exasperating, so as soon as we heard that the *New Racket* had stopped below, somewhere near Kaltag's,

26.—Felling timber for the Yukon steamboats.

we set out in the face of a strong wind. Our canoe frequently dipped water and our headway was slow. This run of 30 miles caused us more work than one twice the distance would have done under favorable circumstances. We reached the *New Racket* at 8 p. m., and were joined by the *Yukon* about midnight, when we started up the river. The former boat had miners' supplies aboard, destined for Fetútlin and Fort Reliance, which it carried for the first time; the latter the usual supplies for the natives.

The Alaska Commercial Company, whose base of supplies for the Yukon River region is Saint Michael's, furnishes the traders their merchandise at 25 per cent. above San Francisco prices, and charges a fixed amount for their transportation up the river. The traders in turn agree to transfer to the company all the furs they obtain at prices which probably do not exceed one-half their value in the San Francisco market. The stations of the different agents are changed as the manager at Saint Michael's sees fit. The station at Anvik was abandoned on this trip, though a few supplies were left with the trader's wife, a half-breed woman. Nuláto was to be abandoned, and through fear lest the natives, incensed at the idea, would offer resistance to the passage of the steamboats, it was decided that both should reach there at the same time; hence the delay of the *New Racket* to await the *Yukon*. Upon our arrival the natives were furious at the intentions of the agent and made some very ugly threats towards the ex-trader, who was finally persuaded, through fear or policy, to leave some supplies with a man, thus making Nuláto a sub-post of Nuklúkyet. The chief agitators here were two half-breeds, Demoósky and Antoósky, who had acted at different times as interpreters to Russian or American traders, and who, knowing the exorbitant prices charged them for their goods, had informed the natives. These became so hostile to the trader that he was unwilling to remain another year. They had not realized that their antagonism might be the cause of the loss of their station until a day or two prior to the arrival of the steamboats.

There were to be but three stations on the Yukon, viz: Fort Reliance, in charge of Messrs. McQuisten and Mayo; Fetútlin, in charge of Mr. Harper; Nuklúkyet, in charge of Messrs. Walker and Fredericksen. These traders have been in the country sufficiently long to know the treatment best adapted to keep the natives friendly disposed; but should the natives become a little more enlightened, as are the half-breeds above mentioned, which they will be as soon as the country is entered by miners and other parties, rebellion against the traders will certainly follow unless better terms be granted by them. The want of clothing by the natives of the Lower Yukon, where skins are scarce, is already the cause of much suffering.

From Nuláto to Nuklúkyet there was continuous rain and the Yukon water was nearly as muddy as that of the Tananá when we descended it. Several stops were made for the purpose of taking on wood, and once, at Nowikákat station, to unload the merchandise destined for it. The illustration represents the natives felling the dead timbers to be used by the steamboats. It is very interesting to watch the natives engaged in an industry comparatively new in their history, and to observe the skill that some of them display. Those living nearest the coast are considered the best laborers, while the value of those farther up is inversely proportional to the distance from the sea. On reaching, Nuklúkyet, July 26, I found, to my surprise, Sergeant Robertson and John in a critical condition from scurvy, and Fickett and Pete looking as though suffering from a severe sickness. The continual fish diet had become nauseating to them and was working disaster by complicating diseases. It was gratifying to see how rapidly the party began to recuperate on wholesome food.

Until the steamboats passed on up the river there was a general uproar, the natives shouting with pleasure one hour, the next threatening the extermination of the whites on the Yukon. Men that had agreed to go with me to the Kóyukuk now deserted me. The Kóyukuks, who were so anxious at first to have me go and to assist me, refused all connection with the undertaking. While at Nuklúkyet I had several conversations with the principal natives through interpreters. They expressed a desire to have schools among them and industries that would give occupation to the young men whereby they could earn money. These expressions I recalled to the quasi chief, "Spot," when his following refused to accompany me to the Kóyukuk. It was not entirely without effect; yet I must give each $1 per day and his food, also canoes for transportation of all from Nuláto back to Nuklúkyet.

27.—WINTER COSTUMES.

NARRATIVE OF KÓYUKUK RIVER.

Having purchased the necessary supplies, I supposed the start for the Kóyukuk could be made without the usual inconveniences incident to the beginning of journeys with Indians. Not so, however; for on the morning of July 28, when ready to move, I found that all but the three smallest Kóyukuks had left Nuklúkyet during the night and that the four Yukon River natives declined to go.

After considerable delay, the necessary number of Indians were obtained, and also two large dogs in addition to the three that had been packed across Miles' Pass. Fickett was the only one of the original party to accompany me. John Bremner and Peder Johnson chose to remain on the Yukon to continue prospecting during the remainder of the summer. They contemplated leaving the country the following year, either by the headwaters of Yukon and over Schwatka Pass to Chilcat, or else by the mouth of the Yukon to Saint Michael's, and trust to the kindness of the commanding officer of the revenue cutter for transportation to the States. Sergeant Robertson was to go to Saint Michael's on the return trip of the steamboat *Yukon*, which was to wait at Nuláto for Fickett and myself until August 23.

There were two ways of reaching the Kóyukuk River that were feasible: one up the Tozikakat in canoes to near its head, thence by a short portage to the Konootená, a tributary of Kóyukuk, and down it to that river; the other by descending the Yukon about six miles, thence by portage nearly N. by E. across the Yukon Mountains of the present charts to the Konootená River, and by descending it as above. When the journey is made during winter, a still different trail is used, starting due north from Nuklúkyet. If the Tozikákat route be traveled it can be reached in canoes via the Yukon, or by a portage to it from Nuklúkyet, the canoes being carried. While at Nuklúkyet I sent out a party of natives to hunt bear on the Tozikákat, and they reached it in the latter manner.

Inasmuch as the Kóyukuks themselves had used the second named route, I decided upon it. One of the barges that had formed part of the tow of the steamboat *Yukon* was left in charge of Mr. Cochrein, to be taken as far as Nowikákat, and in this transportation was obtained to the point of departure on the Yukon River, 6 miles below. I now had 7 natives and 5 dogs packed with food, the average pack of the native being 50 pounds, that of the dog 25. Fickett and myself were in light marching order, carrying only our instruments and weapons. The bedding for both of us consisted of a piece of waterproof linen, the remnant of a sleeping-bag used on the Copper River, and a single blanket.

The description of the hordes of mosquitoes described by Lieutenant Schwatka as existing on the Lower Yukon is not only applicable to those of that part of the Territory, but also to those of the country north of it, even to beyond the Arctic Circle.

Our start for the Kóyukuk was just at the zenith of the " sand fly " season. Why this gnat, which exists where there is not now nor ever was any sand, should be so called, I can only attribute to the astuteness of the pioneers. Some consider them a worse pest than the mosquitoes. There are at least two varieties, differing very much in size.

The party left the Yukon, at the mouth of a very small stream, at 3 p. m., July 28, and in a very short time was ascending to a high ridge, which it endeavored to follow. We were supposed to follow a trail, but if any existed in many places and for long distances it was more than we could detect, though having already had considerable . erperience in such matters. A trail on the plains means quite a different thing from some of the so-called trails of Alaska. The trail from the Copper to the Tananá is in many places well worn, due perhaps to the travel of the moose as well as the natives over it, but the moss over which most of this route lay showed no breaks, save an occasional displacement due to the passing of the party of Kóyukuns who were preceding us. There were many blueberries and a few salmon berries along the way. After a journey of 10 miles we went into camp where a small quantity of timber and water could be obtained. We depended for guides on the Koyukuns, whose efforts seemed to be directed towards following along the high ridges. Upon these the timber is dwarfed and scarce and water obtainable only in small pools. On the highest ridges no vegetation of any description exists.

We left camp the following morning in such a thick fog that a man could barely be seen at a distance of twenty yards. This fog continued all day, accompanied part of the while by rain, all of it by a strong wind from WSW. We halted at 1 p. m. to eat some hard bread, no wood being procurable for cooking. Here we found that we had wandered from our course to the westward. After eating we endeavored to correct our mistake, and at the end of a two hour's march in the fog were at the head of a tributary of the Tozikákat that bore east. The country, except where there is no soil, as along the highest ridges, is covered with a heavy growth of vegetation, such as mosses, lichens, &c. Within a radius of 3 feet I counted eleven different varieties of plants. The rock of the barren ridges is largely fragmentary and granitic, with occasional pieces of nearly pure quartz. Our general course during the early day was, as near as the fog would allow me to determine, N. ½° W.; from noon to the tributary, NNE. A few minutes after sighting the Toziká- kat tributary on our right we came in view of one of the Meloziká- kat on our left and were of course on the divide between them. This we followed in a NE. by N. direction around to NW. by N., and went into camp on a tributary of the tributary recently seen. The heads of all the streams are surrounded by timber, and here we found no exception. Our camp was in a grove of larger timber than any seen since leaving the Yukon. One tree, a spruce, was nearly 2 feet in diameter.

July 30 we left camp in a similar fog to that of preceding day. After traveling an hour beyond tributaries of Tozikákat the coun- try became less marked by ridges, our course being over swampy grounds that characterize so much of the territory of Alaska, even on high elevations. Over this ground the footing is miserable, the hummocks or *têtes de femmes* offer a very uncertain hold for the feet. To walk between them is to walk continually in water of un- even depth, which consequently is very tiresome. The hummocks are covered with grass, moss, bush-birch, or blueberry bushes. Sometimes all of them grow there, with an addition of an occasional very small spruce.

Surrounding our camp was an extensive flat that had comparatively recently been burnt over, and a few small lakes. The cold wind and fog, though disagreeable, were welcomed as a preventive against the gnats and mosquitoes. There was no sign of a trail during the day. The natives unanimously agreed that six more days would be neces- sary to reach the Kóyukuk. They were informed that rations would not be issued at the end of the fourth day. They believed it. We reached the river at the end of the fourth day.

The march of the 31st was quite similar to that of the previous day, except that the swampy grounds were more difficult to cross and the lakes more numerous. In many places for long distances we waded up to our knees. The day's march was about 16 miles and the general direction NNE. ½° N. The ability of the natives to follow a trail and their keenness of eyesight is shown by the following in- cident of the day.

Early in the forenoon the field glasses dropped from their case, but were not missed for probably several hours afterwards. I never ex- pected to recover them, so threw the case to a native. After a few minutes, consultation among themselves it was agreed that one of them should go back for the much-coveted article. I never sus- pected that he would be able to find them and doubted whether he would be able to follow our trail. At 7 o'clock in the evening he was sighted 2 miles in our rear, and an hour later he joined us in camp with the glasses.

Three miles south of camp we crossed a tributary of the Melozi-kákat, the largest seen by us, 40 feet wide and 4 feet deep. Our first efforts were directed towards extemporizing a raft. While engaged in the work, one of the Koyukuns, a deaf-mute, found a fallen spruce tree that was used as a bridge.

August 1 the route lay over higher ground, with better footing. After four hours walking we reached the trail from the Tozikákat to the north, which we followed without difficulty. Three miles farther we crossed a small tributary of the Melozikákat, where the Koyukuns on their visit south had made a *cache* of some meat and fish. From this fact I inferred our portage was about half completed. During the afternoon we crossed yet another tributary of the Melozi-kákat, the last of that much seen river. The last 5 miles of the days' march bore N. 15° W. The distance traveled was 26 miles, the longest march made by us in any one day while in the Territory.

The march the following day was, however, nearly as long. The cold, cloudy weather was favorable to moving along rapidly, while the wind helped to relieve us from the torments of the myriads of gnats and mosquitoes. At the end of the day's march the natives informed us that but two days would be required to reach the Ko-nootená. The following day in the forenoon we were on a ridge from which tributaries of it were visible.

We had crossed the so-called Yukon Mountains and had nowhere seen hills higher than 2,000 to 2,500 feet in height. Their highest points were devoid of snow. From our position were seen two small tributaries, one on each side, emptying into Tatatóntly Lake. The outlet of this lake has the euphoneous name of Mentanóntlekákat. The bearing of the river was N. 3° E. We halted for dinner on its left bank, near a most miserable house used by some Koyukuns during the season of fish in the lake. After dinner we crossed the river and ascended a ridge, from which the lake was visible. Its length is probably 3 to 4 miles. Besides it, 55 small lakes were seen from our prominent position. Our packers were young and anxious to test their own endurance as well as ours; so about 7 o'clock in the evening a running race for a full half hour, packs on the back, was indulged in. They stopped satisfied that we were able to keep apace with them, though I must confess that it was the most stubborn contest I ever engaged in, and more than once I regretted having made the start. The last third of the day's march, 7 miles, was NNE. At 8 p. m. camp was made, the wind was gone, mosquitoes numerous. Our shelter tent of three widths of cotton cloth was thrown over an elongated "wickyup," which was then made mosquito proof by putting moss around the sides and on the edges of the cloth. In this house Fickett and myself nightly sought repose. It was always constructed after the bedding was made down, because it was too low to permit any other order of arrangement.

We left camp August 3 at 5.30, and for four hours trod over a marshy soil to the junction of the Mentanóntlekákat and Konootená Rivers. On arriving there several shots were fired to notify the villagers on the Konootená one-half mile above, of our approach In a few minutes canoes came down the river and we were paddled up it to a village of five men, three women, and five children, situated on its left bank. The river at this place is about 30 yards wide and 5 or 6 feet deep, with a current of 4½ miles per hour, We had made the march from Nuklúkyet, in latitude 65° 8', longitude 152° 30', to Konootená village, in latitude 66" 18', longitude 151° 45', a distance in a right line of 87 miles, by the trail at least 120 miles, in six and a half days. Considering the nature of the footing, this was a very unusual march and could not have been accomplished had not our packs been small and the weather cooler than that of many a day passed on the Yukon. It is a mistaken impression that so far north there can be no warm weather. During the middle of the day in midsummer, when the sun is shining, the heat is felt almost as much as it is in the Middle States.

In running down the Tananá River I was ten days without footgear of any description, and suffered no discomfort. At the village of Konootená, about 10 miles south of the Arctic Circle, likewise at the village of Nohoolchíntná, about 15 miles north of it, nearly all natives were barefooted. While traveling, however, protection of some kind is necessary for the feet.

KONOOTENÁ RIVER TO FICKETT RIVER.

At Konootená we had the usual difficulty in trading with the natives. At last two birch canoes were obtained, the Koyukuns discharged, and with our Yukon natives we started down the stream. After a run of .about 14 miles in a direction NNW. ½° W. we reached the Kóyukuk River, astonished to find such a great volume of water. Before leaving Nuklúkyet the Keyukuns had informed us that its source could be reached by canoe in six days from the mouth of the Konootená. After seeing it with its current of nearly 4 miles per hour, I realized this to be impossible unless its headwaters are the outlets of enormous lakes.

The Kóyukuk, where we first saw it, was in a single channel about 300 yards wide, with high banks, covered with moss and burnt spruce on north side. Accompanying us were three canoes, containing each a man. Later a family, consisting of husband, wife, and small boy, in two canoes, joined us. The head of the family here, as on the Yukon, travels alone in a small canoe, while the wife and children travel in a large one. The two canoes we were using were "squaw" canoes. We immediately adopted the novel system of propelling them used by our traveling companions. We followed along the bank as closely as possible, where the current was least, and with

S. Ex. 125——7

light sticks in hand pushed the canoes forward. Fickett and myself, with two natives each, had a canoe, hence each canoe had three
pairs of sticks for propellers. The sticks were put in the water about
as many times per minute as the average oarsman would put in
his oar in rowing. If properly skilled in the way of using these
sticks there need be no trouble in steering. The bottom of the
Kóyukuk was well adapted for this sort of work, owing to its firm-
ness. Nowhere in the river did we find quicksands. In this respect
it presented a marked contrast to the Copper and Tananá Rivers, and
resembled in many respects that portion of the Yukon between the
Ramparts and Nuláto.

We found the water in the river at a high stage, due probably to
the recent excessive rains. I cannot think that the highest stage of
water is coexistent with the greatest melting of snow on the mountains of its headwaters, for this had taken place several weeks previously.

Camp August 3 was made 7 miles above the mouth of the Konootená, on its south bank, at the foot of a knoll from which high
hills to the northward could be seen. Once, while on the trail, hills
partially snow covered, north of the Kóyukuk and near it, were seen.
With this exception no snow had been seen since leaving Nuklúkyet.
During the night of the 3d, between 8 p. m. and 6 a. m., the river
rose 18 inches. During the day and night of the 4th it fell 24 inches.
It fell 10 inches on the night of August 6; rose 6 inches the following night, 13 the following, and fell 6 the next night. These radical
changes in its stage in such short periods are readily enough
accounted for when it is remembered that the entire face of the
country is covered with a deep moss, nearly as thoroughly saturated
as a wet sponge, and that but a few inches below this is a bed of
rock, frozen ground, or ice that prevents the water sinking. This
condition of affairs exists in a more marked degree the farther north
they are noticed. The rises in the river above considered were all
preceded by rain in our own locality. From the mouth of Konootná
River up to the Allenkákat River frequent islands were passed, the
position of nearly all of which is recorded on the map.

The mouth of Allenkákat is in approximate latitude 66° 37', longitude 151° 16'. Below it is a very high cut bank of clay, called by
the natives Unatlótly. Why this should receive a name when prominent mountain peaks did not I could not ascertain. On the right
bank was a miserable barábarra and a spruce-bough tepee—the one
a winter house, the other a summer one, but neither occupied.

The Indian with family who accompanied us was an old man. He
had, as he said, been more than once over the mountains in which
this tributary heads, to a rather small river, Basnuná, then down it
to a large river, the Holöatná. He mapped out the Allenkákat, showing it to have five tributaries. He said it would require five days

paddling up it before beginning the portage, which would also take five days. The large river to which the portage is made is doubtless the Kówuk, which Lieutenant Cantwell, U. S. Revenue Marine, ascended during summer of 1885, and on which Lieutenant Stoney, U. S. Navy, is now encamped. At the junction it was difficult at first to decide whether the Allenkákat or the Kóyukuk was the larger. The former can be ascended quite a distance in a steam launch, pro_ vided no falls exist. Below the Unatlótly the land on the north side near the river is for 5 miles very low and partly submerged.

We went into camp August 4 on an island 18 miles above last camp and 6 miles above the mouth of Allankákat, where I found a single bone, the *os pubis*, of the mammoth, partially imbedded in the alluvial soil. It was not in position, but had evidently been carried there by the water. It was in a fair state of preservation and to all appearances had never undergone any process of petrification. Here we made a *cache* of 50 pounds of flour and 8 or 10 pounds of bacon. These were made fast to the end of a long cottonwood pole, hoisted and allowed to rest against a standing tree. Other trees were cut so that by falling against the *cache* tree they afforded protection to the provisions and at the same time helped to mark the place.

Along this part of the river the current seemed less than above or below; a short distance above is a decided horseshoe bend with low land on each side. Five miles below Camp August 5 is the small stream Sohjeklakákat, emptying from the north. Mount Cone was visible for first time when near the mouth of this stream. Though probably not more than 2,000 feet high, it is a very prominent landmark in this locality, as is also a double-pointed mountain bearing NNW. This and Mount Cone were all that could be seen from our low position of the ranges to which they belonged. At 8.40 we went into camp thinking we had traveled a distance of 30 miles. When plotted it measured just 20, a discrepancy that frequently occurs, whether the travel be on foot or in boat, whether it be ascending or descending. We left camp in a cold rain storm that continued all day. At 4 p. m. we were at the mouth of the Nohoolchíntna River, on which is situated an Indian village about equal in size to Konootená village, and from the natives' reports is about the same distance from the Kóyukuk as is the former. This is the village towards which our *camarades de voyage*, the Koyukuns, were making. It is about 80 miles by the rivers from Konootená village, and is the last settle- ment on the Kóyukuk, though the river extends probably 200 miles farther. Before permitting the Koyukuns to leave us, further inquiries were made with regard to the headwaters of the river. The old man informed us that it would require three short or two long days' work to reach the Ascheeshná, a tributary emptying on right bank. In this he was right. He claimed that it would require fifteen days to reach the second tributary, Totzunbitná, also flowing in on the right bank. This I doubted, and so expressed myself to the old man, who insisted that he was right, further strengthening his statements by holding up his bare feet and counting the days' marches on his toes. Furthermore, he claimed that it would require thirty days to reach the headwaters of the Kóyukuk. Whether his latter statements be correct is a matter for future explorers to determine.

The other tributaries named in their order by the old man are Klakasiúka and Núzuntotakyúhoo, on left bank; Ezozwátna, on right bank; and Hoochítna, the last tributary or river itself. I have indicated these in dotted lines on the map.

Our dogs could in the future be of no value to us, and on the other hand would consume much food if kept with us, so one was given to the natives, two killed, and two retained to be taken to the States. Having passed the mouth of the Nohoolchíntna, we paddled and poled for two and a half hours to make a distance of 3 miles, where we went into camp. Our Yukon natives, in a strange country, were now becoming very timid, worked indifferently, and begged to be allowed to go back. All refused to eat supper. A few hours after reaching camp three natives from the Nohoolchíntna village joined us, bringing several dogs and one or two king salmon to barter. Their arrival seemed to have somewhat relieved the minds of our Yukon natives, who were willing to eat some breakfast. When it became necessary to leave camp in the cold rain they again became faint-hearted and sullen. During the afternoon we passed high rocky banks on our left, which were of dark sandstone, much broken. Later some islands, above which the river was half a mile wide, were passed.

After making 12 miles we went into camp 8 miles below the north end of Moore Island, in approximate latitude 66° 54', longitude 150° 27'. In the afternoon of the following day we had the first view of snow-covered mountains, the highest of which, as we then saw them, bore about one point south of west. Later the range appeared to have a course east and west. A smaller range of mountains was visible between the river and the snow-covered one, and is quite similar to the highest land between the Yukon and Tananá, and I have called it Beck's Hills. Before going into camp snow-covered mountains became visible anywhere within an area of 50°. Several compass observations of Mount Cone served to locate it. A snow-covered mountain to its east showed Mount Cone to form a peak of the foothills of the principal range. About 10 miles above Moore Island, on the right bank, were the graves of several natives. The river had washed the bank away until the crosses which marked some of them were tottering, ready to fall into the water.

We went into camp on a small island near the foot of Beck's Hills, after having traveled thirteen hours and having ascended the river 23 miles. The channel above the Allenkákat is much more divided by islands than below, and the river has a much more rapid current.

The trees of this locality are indeed dwarfed, and are limited to spruces, cottonwoods, alders, willows, and some birches. Their foliage had already begun to show the effects of frost. This camp was about 67° 10′ latitude, 150° 30′ in longitude. We left the next morning with prospects for a clear day, a cold wind blowing from the snow-covered mountains. About half an hour later we were enabled to get an observation for longitude, the first for several days on account of the rainy weather.

Three miles above camp we were at the mouth of the Ascheéshna or Fickett River. Up to this time no diminution in the volume of water in the river was apparent, notwithstanding we had passed three tributaries, one of which appeared nearly as large as itself. We were beyond the habitations of the natives, in a country of little game, with about 8 pounds of rice and beans, 10 pounds of flour, 3 pounds of bacon, and 2 pounds of lard. It is true we had a *cache* of 60 pounds of food 68 miles below, yet we did not know what to expect before reaching Nuláto. After ascending the Ascheéshna for 5 miles a halt was made to take an observation for latitude at our highest point, 67° 16′. The average width of this river is about 100 to 125 yards, with a depth near its mouth of 14 feet. Having become satisfied that this river would be navigable for many miles, we started down it to halt below its mouth, where the Kóyukuk had 18 to 20 feet of water in it.

We ascended Mount Lookout to get, if possible, the general course of the rivers and the mountains. From its summit, about 800 to 1,000 feet above the river, we obtained a splendid view of the valley of the Ascheéshna and the mountains in which it rises. The extreme mountains whence it comes appeared to be 60 to 80 miles from us in a right-line course. The highest peaks I should judge are about 4,000 feet high and were snow-covered one-third the distance to their bases. The valley presented no marked contrast to other valleys previously described save in the absence of lakes. Its general course is NNE.

The bearing of the farthest visible water of the Kóyukuk from Mount Lookout is NE. by E. For about 6 miles the river bears NE. ½° N., then for about 15 miles it bends towards Mount Cone (bearing E. by N.), thence by many turns to NE. by E. The more abundant growth of timber along the water enabled its course to be approximately traced. The mountains from which it seems to come are much farther away than those of the Ascheéshna, though doubtless the same. They appeared, as far as the eye, aided with field-glasses, could determine, to become lower to eastward, though not to westward. A break in the mountains bearing NE. was seen at a distance of 20 to 30 miles. It is possible that this marks the valley of the Totzunbítna, described by the old Koyukun.

There are no lakes visible on either side of the Kóyukuk. The mountains extended down but a short distance between the two rivers.

FICKETT RIVER TO HUGGIN'S ISLAND.

At 4 o'clock we made for our canoes, glad to get rid of the mosquitoes and sand flies, which were more numerous on the high land than near the water. At 5.30 we started down stream, " bound for home." In a few minutes we met a Mahlemute (Eskimo) in a patched and much-worn canoe, heading for headwaters of the Ascheéshna River, thence over the mountains to where there were " plenty Mahlemutes." Our natives being unable to converse with him, obtained little information. His first request was for cartridges for his old model Winchester rifle, which had been furnished by the Arctic whalers.

As best we could learn, he had been down to Nohoolchíntna on a trading expedition. He had quite a supply of dried salmon, some of which we obtained in exchange for tobacco. Having been informed by the traders from Saint Michael's that Lieutenant Cantwell, U. S. Revenue Marine, would cross from the Kówuk to the Kóyukuk and descend it, I surmised that this old Mahlemute had acted as his guide. It was impossible to make him understand us, so we parted none the wiser on that subject. He had a small skin bag filled with the crystals of iron pyrites, which he brought forth doubtless imagining he had a treasure. When informed that they were valueless he gave them to our boatmen, who carefully carried them to the Yukon.

The run down to the junction of the Konootená was uneventful. On the morning of the 10th we passed some women and children from the Nohoolchíntna, *en route* to the Allenkákat for fish. They were miserably clad and yet worse sheltered from the cold rain. To keep her child warm a mother put it next to her skin, by raising it over her head and dropping it down the enlarged neck aperture of her parkie. From these women we learned that the old Mahlemute we had met the preceding day lived on a tributary of the Holoátna. We went into camp at 6.15 p. m., 2 miles below the Allenkakat, having traveled about 40 miles. We had stopped at our *cache*, which had been undisturbed during our absence. The following morning we were again at the mouth of the Konootená, 468 miles from Nuláto.

As we descended in latitude a marked difference in temperature was observed. We no longer had the cold winds from the snow mountains. At 1 p. m. we went into camp 17 miles below the Konootená and almost due west from it, unwilling to run further without observation for longitude. During the run of August 12 (46 miles) seventeen islands were passed, the largest of which is Waite's Island. * Thirty-seven different courses were followed, the river varying in width from 250 to 400 yards. The map, though

---

* Called in honor of Miss Waite, of Washington City, who has evinced a marked interest in the development of Alaska.

constructed on a scale of 4 miles to the inch, is too small to show all the islands. At 20 miles below mouth of Konootená were high bluffs of dark sandstone. Five miles below the sandstone bluffs appears a very peculiar high red hill, barren of vegetation. It was not unlike some of the buttes of the "Bad Lands" of Dakota and Montana. I have called it Red Mountain.

As we descended broods of young ducks and geese were frequently met with, and our fare correspondingly increased and improved. Above the Nohoolchíntna scarcely a water bird was seen, but from this time forward we succeeded in killing from three to fifteen daily with scarcely any delay, and this while seated in canoes armed with one miserable shot-gun and a carbine. The run of the 13th was 28 miles SW. by S. to approximate latitude 65° 44′. Camp was opposite Huggin's Island,* 14 miles long. Coming in from the north side, Batzakákat River is reported. We could not see it on account of the island. If it exists, it is the only tributary within a distance of 181 miles.

HUGGIN'S ISLAND TO KOTEELKÁKAT RIVER.

Ten miles below our camp we found a summer encampment of natives, Batzakákat, ten in number, including men, women, and children. Their nearest neighbors in an easterly direction are the inhabitants of the Konootená village, 200 miles distant. From these natives we obtained quite a supply of fish, dried during the present season and stored away for winter use. Men, women, and children escorted us to the *cache* on an island 1 mile down stream to see that the bartering was properly done. After leaving Batzakákat village the river runs southwest 15 miles, then northwest 10 miles, with high rock bluffs most of the distance along the right bank. In the middle of the channel is an occasional high, rocky island, partially timber covered. Further the course is west for 8 miles, then west northwest 15 miles. Below this the river runs in a most tortuous course to the Yukon, its meanderings equaling those of the Lower Mississippi. We halted for the night after a run of 63 miles, which put us in longitude 156° 03′. A few miles above our camp the right bank of the river for a short distance was ice, covered with soil to a depth of 4 or 5 feet. The topography of the adjacent country is such as to permit an explanation of its presence similar to that given by either one of two theories laid down in the appendix to "Beechey's Voyage to the Pacific and Behring's Strait." Twenty-five miles below the ice banks the Hogatzakákat empties from the north with a volume of water somewhat less than that of the upper tributaries, on which the villages are situated. A few miles below are high banks

* Named after E. L. Huggins, Captain Second United States Cavalry, for a long time a resident of the Territory and a warm friend of the expedition.

of stone, rich in color, and intersected with small veins of quartz. Twelve miles below the Hogatzakákat River we found a family of Mahlemutes, five in number, encamped on a gravel beach. They were decidedly the most abject, poverty-stricken natives seen since we had left the headwaters of the Copper River. None of the family had clothing of any description from the thighs down, and the small quantity of it they did possess was made of caribou skin, greasy and ragged. Their livelihood was a precarious one, they depended for food chiefly on young water fowls, secured by means of a tri-tined spear. They doubtless had *caches* of dried salmon somewhere in the vicinity, but we saw none. They pointed to the high mountains to the north, indicating at the same time that they would cross them when the litter of pups they were training had grown larger. Their dwelling was the only one of its kind that I saw in the Territory. It was pyramidal in shape and covered in with spruce bark. At a distance it resembled a much-smoked tepee of the Plain Indians, or else the house constructed of drift-timber over the dead by the Mahlemutes of the coast.

At 4 o'clock we were at the beginning of Treat's Island, which seemed to equally divide the water of the river. We were in doubt as to the channel to take. The natives decided the question and we passed along the northern side. The distance traveled by us in passing from its extreme eastern to western point was 28 miles, while the actual right-line distance between the same is but 10. Since plotting the map the natural inference is that we selected the longer route. Along the northern part of this island a portage of 1 mile would have saved travel by water of 12.

We stopped for the night on the island 5 miles above an Indian camp of two men, three women, and six children. Between their camp and ours the Dakliakákat River empties, and from it the trail starts over to the Holoöatna. It has been suggested that if a route be found over the mountains north of the Kóyukuk, it might be used by shipwrecked sailors when unable to reach Saint Michael's by the coast on account of ice. This supposes also the loss of their provisions. The routes exist—in fact, three—but an attempt to reach supplies at Saint Michael's, trusting to food to be procured from the natives along the route, would be fraught with more serious danger than a division of the party and the passing of the winter among the Eskimos.

The most westerly peak of the mountains to the north and near the trail is uniformly pyramidal in shape, and is *doubtless a landmark* to the natives. On the morning of the 16th we passed the mouth of a small stream, Dotlekákat, near which was a camp of Koyukuns, consisting of two men, one of whom was blind, three women, and seven children. In the afternoon a camp of seventeen souls was also passed, the only one whose inhabitants offered to donate

28.—Red Shirt, Koyukun "Medicine Man" and Tyone. (Taken at St. Michael's on a Russian howitzer.

fish. They vied with each other in giving the greatest amount. Yet later in the afternoon we passed another camp of one man, two women, and five children, almost opposite the most northerly end of Cumberland Island. We halted for the night a few miles above the Husliakákat River, the largest tributary south of Allenkákat River. It is 100 yards wide and enters the Kóyukuk almost at a right angle. There is an Indian village situated somewhere on its waters, though its position is not known. Below this tributary the river runs in zigzag courses south to Cawtaskákat River, a distance of 42 miles.

The Doggetlooskat River, 12 miles above the latter, empties from the west in latitude 65° 38'. While its mouth is but 10 miles by land from the most northern point of Colwell Bend, by river it is 40. For two days no mountains were seen on either side of the river save the apparently short range to the northward, containing the pyramidal mountain. The river in places was from 600 to 800 yards wide, its current not greater than 3½ miles. The Cawtaskákat is reported to head in a large lake, around which a few natives live.

Eight miles below the Cawtaskákat and 3 miles below the Dulbekákat is the metropolis of the Kóyukuk River, the home of a famous medicine man, Red Shirt, who was implicated in the massacre at Nuláto in 1851, when Lieutenant Barnard, of Her Majesty's Navy, lost his life. I had met him a few weeks previous, on the Yukon River, *en route* to his home from a trading expedition to Saint Michael's. On arriving at his village we learned that he had gone over the mountains, via the trail of the Dotlikákat, to Kówuk River, to guide Lieutenant Cantwell to the Kóyukuk.

Meeting Lieutenant Cantwell shortly afterwards on the *Corwin*. I learned that he had passed down the Kówuk before the arrival of Red Shirt. This village, numbering forty-five souls, is located on the right bank of the river, in latitude 65° 29', longitude 157° 07'. It is situated at the beginning of the Colwell Bend in the river, the distance across the neck of which is 3 miles, while around by the channel to same point it is 30. In the bend the river is marked by the absence of islands and high hills. On the morning of the 19th we began passing West's Island, following the southern channel, and at night camped a few miles below it at the junction of the Koteelkákat. We were informed that to pass by the northern channel would require a very much longer time.

KOTEELKÁKAT TO NULÁTO.

At the confluence of the Koteelkákat and Kóyukuk Rivers is a small island, on which a summer camp was situated; just across, on the right bank of the Kóyukuk Kiver, below the junction, is the site of the station established shortly after the transfer of the Territory.

It has been abandoned for a number of years. Its position is in latitude 65° 18′, longitude 157° 46′, and is 56 miles from junction of the Kóyukuk and Yukon. This is the highest point reached on the Kóyukuk by Lieutenant Zagoskin, of the Russian Navy, in the winter of 1842, though he ascended the Koteelkákat to latitude 65° 35′. Around the abandoned trading station is an assemblage of three or four winter houses and a number of *caches*, which resemble the villages on the Yukon near the stations.

Thus far in the Kóyukuk region we had been in *terra incognita;* but farther to its mouth white man had preceded us. The mouth of the Koteelkákat is 75 to 100 yards wide, though the river apparently is not very deep. The natives said it was a rather small river, a conclusion to be drawn from the topography of the country. The mouth of the Kóyukuk is almost due south of that of the Koteelkakat, though many bends must be followed to reach it. In latitude 65° the Kóyukuk is but 2 miles from the Yukon, while 16 miles must be traveled by water to that river. Had we known this one of the natives could have been dispatched to Nulato to notify the captain of the steamboat of our near approach, and in consequence the party could have had transportation to Saint Michael's by steamboat instead of by canoe and foot.

Below the Koteelkákat are three small tributaries in the order named: Bitzlatoilóeta, Gissassakakat, and Succosleánty, the last two on the right bank. The river along this portion varies from 500 to 1,000 yards in width, with a current of about 3 miles per hour. On the 20th we passed two camps of natives, about equal in number to those previously mentioned. The trail to the Yukon is in the vicinity of Succosleánty River at the beginning of Nulato Bend, on the most easterly part of which we halted for the night. A few miles above the Succosleánty, on the right bank, are indications of coal-beds, made manifest by pieces of slate coal found at the foot of a " land slide." Some large pieces of it were found that were of inferior quality, and a few small pieces that might be called a fair grade of bituminous coal.

August 21 we left camp on eastern extremity of Nuláto Bend, wondering whether there was an end to the Kóyukuk River. The journey had become very monotonous; the high hills on the left had given away to low lands, showing that the Yukon hills had terminated, while to the west were hills similar to the ones we had seen so much. At noon we halted on right bank, 10 feet above the water, for an observation. Cottonwood trees on this point were scarred to a height of 5 or 6 feet, showing that the river attains at certain seasons a rise of 15 or 16 feet. This would be sufficient to flood a large tract of land on the left bank. The place of our halt was in sight of Kóyukuk Mountain, which touches both Kóyukuk and Yukon water. We did not know at the time of our nearness to the latter river, which we reached at 1.30. At the junction of the rivers is a large island called Yukon Island, between which and Mount Kóyukuk is a distance of 1,200 yards. At 3.30 we halted opposite an island of the Yukon River on which was an Indian camp. In answer to our signal a native crossed over and informed us that the steamboat had passed that point the preceding evening, which naturally made us feel comfortable. A few hours later natives at a fishing camp informed us that the steamboat had left Nuláto bound for Saint Michael's, which announcement was very discomforting, in view of the fact that the *Corwin* might already be at Saint Michael's ready for her departure to San Francisco. About 15 miles above Nuláto, on the right bank, a most excellent opportunity is given to study the crust of the earth for a depth of several hundred feet. The strata has been uplifted and the stratification left nearly normal to the water. We reached Nuláto at 7.30, several hours too late for the steamboat.

NULATO TO SAINT MICHAEL'S.

The steamboat having left Nuláto with a liberal supply of wood, as we learned from the natives, there could be no chnace of over-taking her, so a start was not made until the following morning. Some flour, tea, tobacco, and ammunition were obtained from the small supply of stores left at Nuláto. The latter articles were used as money to purchase fish or such other food as could be found and also to employ help. At Nuláto only one man's services could be secured, notwithstanding liberal offers were made. The four natives who had accompanied us since leaving Nuklúkyet could not be induced to go farther, so they were paid and discharged.

A start down the Yukon with a single native was made at 8 o'clock the following morning. I had hoped by making the portage to Norton Sound to be able to reach Saint Michael's nearly as soon as the steamboat. Had I known that the revenue-cutter *Corwin* would not anchor off Saint Michael's before September 4, there would have been no necessity for forced marches. Her arrival was uncertain; furthermore, the anchorage near was such as not to allow her to remain in the vicinity during the strong winds which frequently occur there.

We called the native we employed "Dandy," which name was quickly taken up by other natives and to which he readily responded. He is the native that murdered the Russian, Iván Kogénikoff, in 1882, though a more peaceable Indian in appearance does not at present live on the Yukon. Dr. George F. Wilson, U. S. A., who accompanied Lieutenant Schwatka, relates the circumstances of the murder as follows:

The Russian, whose name was Iván Kogénikoff, was held in great fear by all the natives, not only on account of his naturally quarrelsome disposition, but on ac-count of the very summary manner in which he had avenged a murder occurring farther down the river some years ago, and many of them would have been delighted at the prospect of disposing of him had they dared. One night he was being liter-ally dragged home in a helpless state of intoxication by an Indian whose brother had been killed by a son of Kogénikoff. The Indian seeing him so utterly helpless and so completely in his power, struck him on the head with an ax, considering the deed justifiable in revenge for the death of his brother.

At the time of his death Kogénikoff was living with Dandy's mother, whom he frequently beat, much to the displeasure of Dandy, who also considered this in the accumulative charges against his stepfather.

Five miles below Nuláto we stopped at a village on the left bank, where I employed the services of the half-breed Demoósky to pack over the trail to the Únalaklík. At 3 o'clock we passed Kháltat's village, on an island in the middle of the river. This is always used as a stopping place in the winter by traders going to and returning from Saint Michael's, a fact that caused our action in paddling by seem highly discourteous to Kháltat. We halted for the night at 7.35 at a small village on the right bank, having experienced the cleansing effects of a rain the entire afternoon. This camp is 65 miles below Nuláto, and is the place where a native acquainted with the trail was obtained to pilot us over the summer portage, the one we traveled, and one which is very little used. Four miles below camp we halted the following morning at an Indian village for "water boots" (seal-skin boots). This is a village on Raymond's chart known as Yakutskalítnik, and consists of six to eight houses. Here I met the messenger I had sent from Nuláto about July 25, returning from Saint Michael's. He had made the journey as Indians usually do, satisfied that time is not an important element in any of their actions. We learned at this village that the natives around Anvik had broken into the store and carried away all the supplies and ammunition left by the trader, Mr. Fredericksen, in charge of his wife. Our hosts inquired what would be done with the transgressors, with whom they evidently sympathized. I here learned that it had been planned by the people all along the river to take possession of all the stores at the several posts. Demoósky said the natives above wanted to do the same, and that probably fear alone prevented. This man is something of a leader amongst them and probably does more than any man on the river, unless it be his ally and fellow interpreter, Antoosky, to encourage them in their rebellion against the traders.

Six miles below Yakutskalítnik we reached the mouth of a small clear stream, the Autokákat, which we ascended 3 miles to the point of departure of the summer trail to the Únalaklík. Here we made a large fire and dried our effects, preparatory to packing them, as much as the then falling rain would permit. We left the Autokákat River at noon and traveled five and half hours over the softest footing until we made camp for the night. Our course for several miles was NW. $\frac{1}{2}°$ W., then it turned more to the northward, so that our camp on high ground was NW. $\frac{1}{2}°$ N. from the mouth of the Autokákat.

The morning of August 24 was clear, and the trail, which presents no appreciable contrast to that from Nuklúkyet north, lay along a high ridge convex to westward. The mosquitoes and gnats form a lively factor in the inconvenience of trail work in this part of the Territory also. At 9 o'clock we halted on summit of high ridge between two tributaries of the Autokákat, one of which we had crossed the preceding day. From this place the trail turns the tributary by making an extended detour.

The principal tributary of the Autokákat bears considerably to west of the trail we followed. The latter part of the day's march was very severe. We had passed to where the ridges have given place to very high hills which necessitated continual ascending and descending. Just before halting for the night we crossed in quick succession three tributaries of a Únalaklík tributary, the cross-section of the largest of which would be represented by 16 by 3 feet.

We had traveled from 7 in the morning until 8.30 at night, including stops, yet I do not think the horizontal distance covered would exceed 14 miles. The following morning on awaking we found a heavy frost resting on all the vegetation, that presented a beautiful picture in the bright sunshine. From a high ridge about 3 miles from camp we first sighted salt water, the only time in my life when such a sight gave me a "home-like" feeling. To our right was the principal tributary of the Únalaklík.

At 2.30 we had a fine view of the valley extending to the sea. At 6 p. m. we crossed the Sessekótna by wading, and at 8.30 went into camp on a high ridge, with no wood save a few scrub alders. The broken mountains, or rather hills, we had been continually ascending and descending were from 1,000 to 2,000 feet in height, and the end of a hard day's march showed but 11 miles to have been traveled.

At noon, August 26, we reached the Únalaklík at the village Úlukuk, situated between two tributaries about equal in size. Efforts were at once made to secure canoes, and the natives, as usual, began the play of "Much Ado About Nothing." These natives are Ingaliks, though all the other inhabitants of the river seen later are Mahlemutes. The method of Ingalik transportation in summer is by small birch canoes, any two of which would have been insufficient to carry our party, together with the dogs ; hence resort was had to a "catamaran" constructed by fastening two canoes to each other a foot and a half apart, their axes parallel. In this craft we left the old man's village about 2 o'clock p. m. There was a current of about 4 miles per hour notwithstanding the very meandering course of the stream. A small stream was passed on each bank before halting for the night at 9.30, on the right bank, opposite a small tributary. At 7.30 the following morning we sighted a village of Mahlemutes, consisting of six men, with corresponding number of women and children, all living in tents. Here we saw baidárras and baidárkas, the kind used on Norton Sound. The patriarch of the village joined us to share our fortunes and misfortunes, but more especially the food we had. In his language I detected a number of words used also by the natives of Nuchek. At this time I supposed the latter natives to be Aleuts, hence wondered much at the similarity.   Two miles below the village is a small tributary on the right bank.

Our craft required frequent repairs, all of which were made by hauling it ashore, turning it bottom upwards, and adding more pitch to the leaks, or else melting the old pitch so that it would run into the defective places.   We halted at noon, where we saw a woman and child a short distance from the bank, supposing a settlement of some kind was near.   Investigation showed a huge barrel and peculiar kind of tub filled with salmon berries in a state of fermentation and covered with small willows.   Near at hand were two young dogs tied with willow sprouts.   The woman and child had disappeared, doubtless frightened at our appearance.   At 2.30 we arrived at the mouth of the Amiklóna River, on the right bank near the junction of which was a Mahlemute village of eight men.   On the left bank of the Únalaklík and nearly opposite is another village, about one-third as large, at the junction of another tributary.   As the coast is approached the river becomes wide and the current sluggish.   The mouth of it is divided into several channels, and the adjacent country for quite a distance from the coast is as flat as the prairies.   The village Únalaklík, reached at 4 p. m., is situated on right bank, on the coast, and is constructed entirely of drift timber, vast piles of which cover the beach.   The village is indeed a curious spectacle, about half of each house being under ground and their roofs covered with soil and rank vegetation.

The smell of fish, seal oil, &c., was sufficient to cause an investigation of their store rooms.   Large quantities of each, also berries, were found stored away in the semi-subterranean houses.   The village was capable of containing several hundred natives, and doubtless does in the winter time, when all the bands are assembled. This village offers a most interesting place for studying the ethnology of the Mahlemute.   Unfortunately, we found but two men here, one of whom I sent to Saint Michael's with a note to commander of the cutter *Corwin*, the other up to the villages recently passed on the Únalaklík, to secure a baidárra and crew with which to travel to Saint Michael's, about 55 miles distant by the coast.   We went into camp under a baidárra 40 feet long that we found on the bank of the slough behind the village.   About 3 p. m. the following day the natives arrived from up the river with a baidárra, much in need of repairs, and a crew of but two men.   A few hours later a similar kind of boat was seen in the direction of Saint Michael's.   While still making our preparations the baidárra recently sighted landed, bringing us the welcome news that it was at our disposal and that the cutter had not been sighted at Saint Michael's.   Mr. Lorentz, of the Alaska Commercial Company, had directed the Mahlemute in charge to put the boat at our disposal should we so desire.

From Unalaklík Saint Michael's bears about WSW.   After getting several natives besides the two from Nuláto, we left the 29th of

29.—Eskimos of Unalaklik River, members of our crew.

August with an unfavorable wind for us. When about a mile out the wind and heavy surf on the bar we were passing threw the natives into such a consternation that with difficulty they were prevented from returning. A few miles farther we ran to the beach at a small settlement to enable a new member of the crew to get in. We paddled and sailed until 5 p. m., when it was found that the excellent footing along the beach was favorable to cordelling, a faster method of traveling than paddling and sailing.

Our baidárra was 36 feet long, 7 feet wide, and 2 feet 9 inches deep, rigged with a single square sail, *à la Mahlemute*. At 4 o'clock the following day we were at a village called Kegiktówruk, and at 8.30 at Saint Michael's, where we remained until September 5, when we started for San Francisco via Ounalaska. Mr. Lorentz, chief trader for the Yukon country, did all in his power to make the party comfortable during its stay at Saint Michael's, and. furthermore, granted us the use of his photographic instrument and plates.

H. Ex. 125——8

PART III.

THE MAPS.

TABLES OF DISTANCE.

THE MAPS.

The most valuable map extant of the interior of Alaska is that compiled by Dall in 1884 "from all accessible data," and printed by the Coast and Geodetic Survey. This includes the work in the interior of the Territory of a number of persons, among whom are Dall and other members of the Western Union Telegraphic Expedition, Raymond, Schwatka, Ray, the Krause brothers, Nelson, Petroff, and others.

The maps forwarded with this report include one each of the Copper, Tananá, and Kóyukuk Rivers, and one representing part of the Yukon River and the Únalaklík; also a general map.

Accuracy cannot be expected of a survey executed in the hasty manner in which this was, yet I think the great care taken to secure a correct geographical description of the rivers will prove them to be of much practical value. The topography of the country away from the rivers could not be attempted, except in the most general way, yet I am sure that the delineation of the mountain system will be found more nearly correct than on any previous chart.

Each of these maps is constructed on a polyconic projection from tables published by the Bureau of Navigation, and, with the exception of the general map, on a scale of 1 inch to 4 miles, or $\frac{1}{253440}$.

On the map of Copper River the one hundred and forty-fourth meridian has been used as the central one, on the Tananá the one hundred and forty-seventh, on the Kóyukuk the one hundred and fifty-second, and on the Únalaklík the meridian of Nuláto.

I have previously spoken of inaccuracies in the determination of longitude due to the non-uniform rate of the watch. The observations for it were made by Private Fickett, while I recorded them. To avoid the effects of errors as much as possible we rated the watch at Tarál, Nuklúkyet, and at Saint Michael's, and reduced the observations taken at intermediate points by using rates determined in rear and advance. When the results differed, as they nearly always did, a longitudinal position somewhere between the two was used. Its nearness to one or the other was given in accordance with the adjudged correctness of the rates. At best the longitude is only approximate, but in the determination of latitude, time being a very small function, the results are more reliable. The latitudinal obser-

117

vations are necessarily a check on the courses determined by compass bearings, and the latter helped to check those for longitudes, while the reverse of the last statement should properly be the case.

Throughout the entire journey the exact time consumed on each course and the direction of that course were recorded. Our rate of travel, whether by foot or by boat, was necessarily estimated. Had we simply floated down the streams the rate could have been fairly accurately obtained by measuring the swiftness of the current; but the value of our paddling, more or less spasmodic, had to be estimated. At all times the tendency was to overestimate, and in plotting some of the distances needed to be reduced one-half. Four hundred and forty-one compass bearings were used in plotting the Kóyukuk River alone and proportionately nearly as many for the other rivers.

The Copper River, as shown on the charts, is included between the sixty and one-half and sixty-third parallels and between the one hundred and forty-second and one hundred and forty-seventh meridians, and drains approximately 25,000 square miles. The Tananá, as shown, is included between the sixty-two and one-half and sixty-fifth parallels and between the one hundred and forty-two and one-half and one hundred and fifty-second meridians, and drains approximately 45,000 square miles. The Kóyukuk is included between the sixty-fifth and sixty-eighth parallels and between the one hundred and forty-seventh and one hundred and fifty-seven and one-half meridians, and drains approximately 55,000 square miles. The relations that these numbers bear to each other express the approximate ratio of the volumes of water discharged by these rivers. Chart III, besides representing the Kóyukuk River, includes the Yukon from the mouth of the Tananá to Nuláto, drawn largely from field observations of the party. Chart IV contains the Yukon from Nuláto to Yakutskalítnik and the Únalaklík, drawn entirely from field notes of the party.

The general chart includes nearly all that portion of Alaska north of the sixtieth degree of latitude and west of the one hundred and thirty-seventh degree of longitude, and is drawn to a scale of 1 inch to 15 miles, or $\frac{1}{950400}$. The one hundred and fifty-second has been used as the central meridian, and, inasmuch as the rivers from the other charts have been reduced to conform to the proper scale, without any allowance for the positions of their central meridians, the relative positions of the rivers are not exactly what they should be.

The chart of the Coast and Geodetic Survey has been followed for coast line and in other respects, while Raymond's and Schwatka's charts are chiefly the authorities for the Yukon.

I am sorry not to be able to include in this chart the results of the work of Lieut. J. C. Cantwell and Assistant Engineer S. B. McLenigan, of the United States revenue steamer *Corwin*, who explored in

1885, respectively, the Kówuk and Nówatak Rivers. From the former's report the lake source of the Kówuk (67° 1′ latitude, 153° 30′ longitude) is taken.

An outline map of the entire Territory has been constructed on a convenient place on the general chart on a scale of 50 miles to the inch.

TABLES OF DISTANCES.

DISTANCES ON THE COPPER AND CHITTYNÁ RIVERS.

Locality.	Description and position.	Preceding locality.	Núchek.	Alagánik.	Tarál.
		Distances from—			
Núchek	On Hiñchinbrook Island, 432 miles west of Sitka.				
Skátalis	Summer village of two houses near the western mouth of Copper River.	46	46		
Alagánik (Anahánuk)	Village of five houses near the western mouth of Copper River.	4	50		
Child's Glacier	Largest glacier, right bank, beginning of Abercrombie Cañon.	28	78	28	
Miles's Glacier	Largest glacier of Copper River, left bank, lat. 60° 44′, long. 145° 33′.	2	80	30	
Camp April 2	Northern end of Abercrombie Cañon, on rocks in the middle of the channel.	6	86	36	
Baird's Cañon	High bluff on left bank, vegetation-covered glacier on right.	8	94	44	
Bremner River	Mouth on left bank, lat. 61° 2′, long. 145° 30′	14	108	58	
Tasnuná River	Mouth on right, lat. 61° 5′, long. 145° 27′, opposite Cottonwood Island.	5	113	63	
Konsiná River	Small stream on right bank	10	123	73	
Zeikhell River	Small stream on right bank, lat. 61° 19′, long. 145° 46′.	11	134	84	
Spirit Mountain	Left bank, Camp August 7	10	141	94	
Wood's Cañon	Southern end	13	157	107	
Tarál	Midnóosky village of two houses, site of an old Russian trading-post, lat. 61° 38′, long. 145° 6′.	5	162	112	
Chittyná River	Mouth on left bank	2	164	114	
Midnóosky Creek	Mouth on right bank Chittyná	11	175	125	13
Dora River	Mouth on right bank Chittyná, lat. 61° 24′, long. 144° 17′, Camp April 14.	18	193	143	31
Chittystone River	Mouth on right bank Chittyná, lat. 61° 22′, long. 143° 51′, Camp April 16.	22	215	165	53
Camp April 17	Beginning of trail to Nicolai's	6	221	171	59
Junction of central and southern branches.	Visible from high point of trail, about 18 miles	18	239	189	77
Camp April 18	On trail to Nicolai's, midway between Chittyná and Chittystone Rivers.	18	239	189	77
Nicolai's house	Left bank Chittystone River, lat. 61° 26′, long. 143° 17′.	13	252	202	90
	From Nicolai's house to mouth of Chittystone via the river is 58 miles.				
Messála's house	Messála River, left bank of Copper		178	128	16
Liebigstag's village	Liebigstag's River, opposite on left bank, lat. 61° 57′, long. 145° 45′.	24	202	152	40
Coneguánta's village	Summer houses on left bank, winter houses on right, lat. 62° 10′, long. 146° 30′.	31	233	183	71

Table of distances—Continued.

DISTANCES ON THE COPPER AND CHITTYNÁ RIVERS—Contin:ed.

Locality.	Description and position.	Distances from—			
		Preceding locality.	Níchek.	Alagánik.	Tarál.
Klatená River	On right bank, 1 mile below Klawasiná	10	243	193	81
Tezliná River	On right bank, heads in Lake Plaveznie of the Russians.	12	255	205	93
Tonkiná River.	On right bank, lat. 62° 32′, long. 146° 40′	25	280	230	118
Gakoná River	On right bank	9	269	239	127
Sanford River	On left bank Torrent, lat. 62° 44′, long. 146° 22′	32	321	271	159
Chitsletchiná River	On right bank	16	337	287	175
Camp May 30	On left bank, beginning of trail to Batzulnéta's.	17	364	304	192
Camp June 1	Near left bank of Copper River, on the trail	29	382	383	221
Batzulnéta's village	On Batzulnéta's Creek, 4 miles from its mouth, lat. 62° 58′, long. 145° 22′.	10	393	343	231
Lake Suslóta	A reservoir of Slaná River, a tributary of Copper.	10	403	353	241

DISTANCES ON TANANÁ RIVER.

Locality.	Description and position.	Distances from—			
		Preceding locality.	Nuklúkyet.	Nandell's.	The sea.
Tananá River	Mouth, left bank of Yukon River		18	548	684
Harper's Bend	Southern part	26	44	522	710
Old Station (Harper's)	Abandoned on right bank, lat. 64° 47′, long. 151° 14′.	22	66	500	732
Summer village	Mouth of Toclat River, left bank	19	85	481	751
Lorentz River	Mouth, left bank, 2 miles below Baker Creek, on right bank.	12	97	469	763
Dugan River	Mouth, left bank	26	123	443	789
Camp June 22	Right bank, lat. 64° 44′, long. 149° 37′	14	137	429	803
Cantwell River	Left bank, fishing station, 4 miles above small stream on left.	35	172	394	838
Camp June 21	Right bank, 2 miles above small stream on left.	8	180	386	846
Summer village	Right bank, 3 miles below small stream on left.	25	205	361	871
Camp June 20	Right bank, river very wide. Probable head of navigation.	22	227	339	893
Delta Creek	Two miles below camp. Head of navigation, lat. 64° 18′, long. 147° 51′.	38	265	301	931
Delta River	Left bank	25	290	276	956
Volkmar River	Largest tributary, right bank	10	300	266	966
Mason's Narrows	Small streams above and below on opposite sides	5	305	261	971
Camp June 18	Right bank, lat. 64° 13′, long. 146° 39′	11	316	250	982
Goodpaster's River	Right bank, second tributary in size	12	328	238	994
Gerstle River	Left bank	4	332	234	998
Camp June 17	Lat. 64° 8′, long. 145° 54′, in Johnson Rapids	24	356	210	1,022
Johnson River	Left bank, head of Carlisle Rapids	26	382	184	1,048
Tower Bluff Rapids	Lower part, Camp June 16	24	406	160	1,072

Table of distances—Continued.

DISTANCES ON TANANÁ RIVER—Continued.

Locality.	Description and position.	Distances from—			
		Preceding locality.	Nukláikyet.	Nandell's.	The sea.
Robertson River	Left bank, opposite Tower Bluffs and head of rapids.	29	435	131	1,101
Cathedral Bluffs	Right bank	15	450	116	1,116
Kheeltat River	Right bank, trail to Fetúliin	10	460	106	1,126
Mentasta Trail	Left bank, also beginning of trail to Nandell's	6	466	100	1,132
Tokái River	Left bank	40	506	60	1,172
Camp June 14	Left bank, lat. 63° 32', long. 143° 58'	8	514	52	1,180
Tetling River	Left bank	32	546	20	1,212
Tetling's house	On Tetling River	9	556	11	1,221
Nandell's house	Nearly south of Tetling's	11	566	0	1,232

Nandell's to Wolverine Gorge (north side Alaskan Mountains), 9 miles.

Wolverine Gorge to Lake Suslota=distance across Miles Pass, 49 miles.

Middle point of Miles Pass=1,265 miles from the sea via the Tananá and Yukon Rivers.

Middle point of Miles Pass=384 miles from the sea via the Copper River.

DISTANCES ON THE KÓYUKUK RIVER.

Locality.	Description and position.	Distances from—			
		Preceding locality.	Nuláto.	Fickett River.	The sea.
Nuláto	Right bank of Yukon			556	467
Kóyukuk River	Mouth on right bank of Yukon, lat. 64° 44', long. 158° 10'.	24	24	532	491
Nuláto Bend	Most eastern part, Camp August 20	16	40	516	507
Indian Village	Left bank, 4 miles below Bitzloitócla River	20	60	496	527
Koteelkákat River	Mouth right bank, abandoned station, Indian village, lat. 65° 18', long. 157° 45'.	20	80	476	547
West's Island	Most southerly point	4	84	472	551
Do	Most northerly point	28	112	444	579
Camp August 18	Right bank	8	120	436	587
Colwell Bend	Most northerly part	14	134	422	601
Red-Shirt's village	Right bank, lat. 65° 29', long. 157° 15'	16	156	406	617
Cawtaskákat River	Left bank, Camp August 17	10	160	396	627
Doggetloóskat River	Right bank	11	171	385	638
Hussleakátna	Right bank, 2 miles above southern end of Dall's Island.	31	202	354	669
Dall's Island	Upper end	9	211	345	678

Table of distances—Continued.

DISTANCES ON THE KÓYUKUK RIVER—Continued.

Locality.	Description and position.	Preceding locality.	Nuláto.	Fickett River.	The sea.
		Distances from—			
Treat's Island	Western extremity	8	219	337	786
Daklikákat River	Right bank, north of Treat's Island, near trail leading to Kówuk River.	12	231	325	798
Camp August 15	On Treat's Island, lat. 66° 3′, long. 156° 40′	6	237	319	804
Treat's Island	Eastern extremity	10	247	309	814
Hogatzakákat River	Right bank	21	268	288	835
Camp August 14	Left bank, lat. 65° 53′, long. 156° 3′	14	282	274	849
Ice-banks	Right bank	17	299	257	866
Barnard Island	Two miles long	24	323	233	890
Batzakákat	Indian village, right bank, western extremity McQuisten's Island.	24	347	209	914
Camp August 13	Left bank, opposite McQuisten's Island	8	355	201	922
Twin Islands	Each about 3½ miles long	14	369	187	936
Camp August 12	Left bank, lat. 66° 3′, long. 153° 57′	14	383	173	950
Waite's Island	Northern extremity	17	400	156	967
Red Mountain	Right bank	10	410	146	977
Camp August 11	On left bank just above Eight-mile Bend	36	446	110	1,013
Konootená River	Left bank	17	463	93	1,030
Mayo Island	Mayo Bend	8	471	85	1,038
Allenkákat River	Right bank, lat. 66° 39′, long. 151° 35′	13	484	72	1,051
Sojeklakákat River	Right bank	23	507	49	1,074
Fish Island	Mouth Nohoolchíntná River, on left bank	9	516	40	1,083
Camp August 7	On right bank (ascending the river)	15	531	25	1,098
Moore's Island	North end	18	539	17	1,106
Mount Lookout	Near right bank, Camp August 8	15	554	2	1,121
Fickett River	Right bank, lat. 67° 10′, long. 150° 30. The mouth of the Konootená=125 miles by trail from Nuklúkyet. The highest point reached on Fickett River =99 miles from mouth of Konootená.	2	556	0	1,123

DISTANCES ALONG THE YUKON AND SUMMER ROUTE TO SAINT MICHAEL'S.

Locality.	Description and locality. (Distances above mouth of the Tananá are taken from reports of Raymond and Schwatka.)	Preceding locality.	Nuklúkyet.	Saint Michael's via the trail.	Crater Lake, head of Yukon.
		Distances from—			
Nuklúkyet	Seventeen miles below mouth of Tananá			419	1,287
Dep. of trail to Kóyukuk	Right bank	6	6	413	1,293
Gold Mountain	Right bank, lat. 65° 5′, long. 153° 43′	35	41	378	1,323
Nowikákat River	Left bank, 2 miles below trading-post	24	65	354	1,352
Melozikákat River	Right bank	42	107	312	1,394
Little Mountain	Left bank, near Little Mountain Island	57	164	255	1,451
Kóyukuk River	Right bank	13	177	242	1,464

Table of distances—Continued.

DISTANCES ALONG THE YUKON AND SUMMER ROUTE TO SAINT MICHAEL'S— Continued

Locality.	Description and locality. (Distances above mouth of the Tananá are taken from reports of Raymond and Schwatka.)	Distances from—			
		Preceding locality.	Nuklúkyet.	Saint Michael's via the trail.	Crater Lake, head of Yukon.
Nuláto	Right bank	24	201	218	1,488
Khaltag's house	..... do	32	233	186	1,520
Autokákat River	Right bank, lat. 63° 45′, long. 159° 10′. Pt. dep. for Únalaklík River.	43	276	143	1,563
Beginning of trail	Left bank of Autokákat	3	279	140	1,566
Camp August 24	On the trail, lat. 63° 56′, long. 159° 57′	29	302	111	1,595
Úlukuk	Ingalik village, between branches of Únalaklík River.	14	322	97	1,619
Únalaklík	Innuit village, mouth of Únalaklík River	42	364	55	1,661
Fort Saint Michael's	On Island of Saint Michael's	55	419	0	1,716
	The Yukon River is navigable as far as Miles Cañon, which is 1,784 miles from its mouth (Aphoon Outlet), 818 miles above Fort Yukon, and 327 miles above Fort Selkirk. The length of the river above Fort Yukon is 989 miles; below Fort Yukon to mouth (Aphoon Outlet) is 963.				

PART IV.

NATIVES.

THE NATIVES.

Upon examination of the natives of Copper River it is found that they are as a rule between 5 feet 6 and 5 feet 8 inches in height, though occasionally a man fully 6 feet is seen, and weigh about 140 pounds; that the color of their skin is a brown, tinged with copper, and much darker than that of their nearest coast neighbors; that their hair is generally straight, exceptionally wavy; and that their eyes are invariably black or nearly so. A great difference in mobility of countenance was noticed, the faces of some being nearly as capable of indicating emotions as those of a civilized people, whilst those of others are almost entirely devoid of expression under any circumstance. Their muscular strength is not so remarkable as their ability to travel great distances in a short time on scanty rations. Ample opportunity was given for measuring their strength and endurance with those of our party. The result of the first few days' work was favorable to them, but ever afterwards to us. It is true, however, that our party was selected with special view to physical strength.

It is an unusual occurrence to see a father and mother with more than three children. Whether this smallness of family be due to the hardships incident to the gaining of a livelihood or to malpractice in some of its forms, I am unable to say. As a fact that with them, too, poverty may be blessed with children, I will instance that one of the most destitute families met consisted of father, mother, and four children, some of whom were sadly emaciated by hunger.

The nature of their food causes so much wearing of the teeth that children are found with the first set worn almost to the gums; with adults the teeth are worn down to the gums while the body is yet in its prime.

The faces show the result of subjection to hardships long before the hair begins to turn gray. Owing to their ignorance of methods of computing time, I was unable to ascertain anything definite relative to their ages. Messála, however, who lives on left bank of Copper, one day's march from Tarál, and presumably led the party of massacre against the Russians in 1848, was then a man of years and influence.

The only sickness noticed among them was due to costiveness, which doubtless disappears as soon as the run of salmon arrives. But one natural deformity was observed—a shriveled leg—yet the toes of nearly all are abnormally crooked from snow-shoe travel.

127

Their sagacity in following trails and hunting game is probably not greater than that of others of the Tinneh family, but would astonish one not accustomed to the skill of natives in this respect.

All the people of the Copper River region were called by the Russians Midnoóskies (more properly Midnóvtsi), and all belong to the great Tinneh family, which peoples the interior of Alaska. Those below the Tezliná River, from their association with Russians, have adopted some abbreviated form of the same, such as Minúsky, Minoósky, &c., while those above it style themselves Tatlatáns. I think the name Atnatána, the Indian name for an inhabitant of Atna (Copper) River region, would be a fitting term for the people of both tribes, who differ very little from each other. To particularize, I have used the term Midnoósky for the people south of the Tezliná, including those living on the Chittyná, and Tatlatán for those living north of the Tezliná.

The entire number of natives on the river and its tributaries is about 366, divided as follows: Men, 128; women, 98; children 140. Between Alagánik and Wood's Cañon, a distance of 110 miles, there are no settlements, yet an occasional party goes down to Bremner River to hunt moose. On the Chittyná and its tributaries are about 30 souls; on the headwaters of Tezliná and Lake Plavéznie, probably 20. The Tatlatáns, including the settlement at Lake Suslóta, number 117. On the Copper, including tributaries between Tarál and the Tezliná, are 209, the total number of Midnoóskes. Nicolai is autocrat of the Chittyná River and the fishing rendezvous. Tarál, whilst between the latter place and the Tezliná this privi- is exercised by Liebigstag and Conequánta, the former controlling the lower part; the latter, with the largest following of any Atna-tána, the upper. The chief native among the Tatlatáns is Batzulnéta, who is a shamán.

As far as I am able to judge from the scanty records of the Russians and my own observations, I should say that the change in number of these people has been very slight for many years. Their history, so far as *their* records are concerned, will always be a sealed book. On both banks of the river between Chittyná and the Klawah-siná River, more especially on the left bank, are frequent excavations 2 to 4 feet, indicating the sites of houses. The more recent of these show signs of the attached bath-house. In some older ex-cavations spruces of the largest size are growing.

The territory of the Atnatánas is included between the one hundred and forty-second and one hundred and forty-seventh meridians and between the sixty and half and sixty-third parallels, representing an approximate area of 25,000 square miles, all of which is drained by the Copper and its tributaries. Practically excluded from the rest of the world, it is but natural that they should be a conservative people. With mountains on all sides, their routes of travel are chiefly confined to the water-courses winter and summer. Were it practicable to pass from Tarál to the upper waters of the Copper by going nearly due north, one-half the distance over the river route which is and must be followed would be avoided. Between these localities are some of the highest mountains of the northern continent, and certainly the highest volcano (Wrangell); below Tarál are huge glaciers. Miles' and Child's, which hem in the river, rendering navigation extremely dangerous. Besides these geographical considerations, the climate, which is practically seven months severe winter, affects in a large measure the customs of the people.

Their vegetable products are limited, scanty in variety and in quantity. Besides the berries, including cranberries, blueberries, a small red berry (called by them *giniss*), a small black berry (called by them *gizneh*), quite similar to the red one, is a fruit called *tombá*, that grows on a bush several feet high. It hangs on the bushes all winter, and may be eaten in the spring, even to summer, when it is very dry and nearly tasteless. The shape and nature of the fruit is very similar to the black haw, though it is of a yellowish-white color. The natives fry it in moose or other fat, at the same time mashing it well with a stick or spoon, thus making of it a palatable dish. Their chief vegetable food, however, is a peculiar parsnip-shaped root, but longer than that vegetable, which they call *chass*. The portion of it above ground is not more than 6 to 12 inches and not unlike a bunch of small willows, while the root is frequently several feet long. It is never cured, but is eaten raw, boiled, or roasted.

Fish, rabbit, moose, sheep, caribou, bear, goat, porcupine, beaver, lynx, muskrat, goose, duck, and grouse constitute the mass of their food. Of these fish is decidedly the most important, with rabbits next in order. They have no process of curing save that by drying in the sun. The fat of the moose is melted and run into the smaller intestines, while the blood is saved in the paunch. It is of little importance to them whether or not their meat be cooked, and in boiling it is seldom allowed to become done through. The entire entrails of rabbits are boiled, sometimes with the bodies from which they were taken, again with other meat, and form one of the most potent anti-scorbutics used by them. Good or special food is always cooked by the men, and the refuse of all is given to the women. A boy five or six years old has precedence at meals over his mother. There seems to be almost no limit to the amount of food a hungry native can consume (and our experience when compelled to live as they do was in no respect different). A single kind of food must be abundant to furnish in sufficient quantities the necessary elements required by the system. A much less quantity of mixed food satisfies. Like most other Indians, they seem to eat when hungry, without regard to fixed intervals.

S. Ex. 125——9

The only drink that I saw used by them, excepting tea, of which they are passionately fond, and the liquors in which the food is boiled, was made from the plant (lamb kill?) used by nearly all the Tinneh of Alaska and by the inhabitants of the Hudson Bay country and Labrador. No special preparation of this is required, not even drying being necessary before using.

If they possess any medicinal preparations or medicines of any description they are in the hands of the shamans, who keep them carefully concealed. Their limited contact with the Russians and Americans, though very slight, has taught them the benefits of more civilized remedies, and they will take any dose given them by a white man.

The houses of the Atnatánas are of two kinds, viz, permanent and temporary. The former are intended for winter use and are annually occupied during that season, while the latter are extemporized at any place where game may be found. The photograph of the house at Tarál fairly represents the winter house of an Atnatána. In plan it is about 18 feet square, is built of spruce poles and slabs in a loose style, and is covered in with spruce bark. In some places moss is used to help to make it close. The walls under the eaves are nearly 4 feet high; about 3 feet from the ground around the inside is built a shelf 4 or 5 feet wide, which serves the double purpose of a seat during the day and bed at night, the space under this being boxed in with vertical slabs and used as a store-room and sleeping apartments for women, children, and pups. The roof is provided with a large hole in the middle, to permit the escape of smoke from the open fire on the floor. The entrance to the house is through a small "storm shed" about 2 by 3 feet, protected at the outer end by an undressed sheep or goat skin. Opposite this at the other end, near the floor, is a round hole about 15 inches in diameter, which is the entrance to the sleeping-room and bath-house. This is about 10 feet square and 4 or 5 feet in height, nearly all of which is under ground, and is lighted by a small aperture over which the intestines of the bear are stretched. The sweat bath is so highly prized that every permanent house of the Midnoóskies and most of those of the Tatlatáns are supplied with the necessary room, the heating of which is quite simple. A large pile of stones placed on a close frame of logs in the main room, after the manner of an old-fashioned lime-kiln, are heated, then transferred to the sweat room by means of two sticks used as tongs. The circular aperture is closed with a kind of *tompion* and water is then poured on until the necessary amount of heated vapor is obtained. *The idea* of building this adjunct to the houses came through contact with the Russians, with whom it is a religious as well as a hygienic measure, and is practiced as far north as the Alaskan Range. Beyond this it is not seen until the Lower Yukon is reached. The temporary or hunting house, always built of poles and boughs of spruce, cotton-

11.—A Midnoosky House.

wood, &c., is rectangular in plan, with a passage-way through the center. Two sides only are used, and in consequence the ends and upper part are scantily covered. A log placed on the fire extends sometimes several feet beyond each end. A moose or caribou skin, in lieu of cotton cloth used by their more civilized brethren, is occasionally used to help make it water-proof directly over the sleeping places. Tents are not as yet part of their possessions, nor is metal of any kind employed in assembling the different parts of the houses, willow withes and rawhide thongs answering their present requirements for this purpose. In general, the winter house, being on the river, may be said to be occupied during the salmon season, and until February, when the occupants depart for the headwaters of streams, where they hunt and trap and improvise summer houses.

Never have I seen Indians more devoid of luxuries than are the Atnatánas. The wealthiest count only the following vessels and utensils in their subsistence departments: One to three large kettles, one tea-kettle, one frying-pan, several wooden trays (native), several knives, generally home manufactured, horn spoons, and two or three cups. In but one place did I see any pretense of furniture, and that was a peculiarly made box to put the tea-cups on. The average head of family dispenses with all the above save one kettle, one or two wooden trays, a knife or two, and possibly a small cup, which he invariably carries whilst traveling. I found no vessels for boiling or holding water that had been used prior to the introduction of modern ones.

Their clothing consists ordinarily of two garments, trousers and boots forming one, coat or parkie the other. In the winter this is sometimes supplemented by a shirt made of rabbit skin. The coat is usually without a hood attachment, differing in this respect from that of the Eskimos, the head-dress being made from marmot or squirrel skins. The principal decorations of the wearing apparel is of beads of which those one-eighth to one-quarter of an inch in diameter are especially prized. Very seldom are porcupine quills utilized for ornamentation.

The men have both ears and nose pierced, the women the former only. In the nose rings made of shell or metal are worn, some of which are 1½ inches in diameter. Sinew suspends the ear ornaments, which are made of elongated beads. To be thoroughly *en règle*, a little red paint must be applied to the face. This applies more particularly to the women and children than to the men. Nicolai alone was never seen to use paint or ornaments of any description; he preferred to adopt the style of the white men. The beaded knife scabbard attached to the neck is considered indispensable to the well-equipped Atnatána, who does not take it off day or night. In addition to this, the tyones and wealthy men wear a beaded ammunition pouch. Bracelets and finger-rings, likewise tattooing, are almost unknown to them. Combs made of the hoofs of the moose are owned by some, while many keep the hair in condition by dexterous use of the hands. They are very fastidious with respect to the hair, which, be it said to their credit, nearly always appears neat, a shaman's excepted. That of the women and shamans is worn long, while many of the men in early summer cut it straight around at the height of the middle of the neck.

The unit of measurement with them is the distance between the tips of the fingers, the arms horizontally outstretched. I have frequently seen them measuring timber for a baidárra or the length of rope or thongs with this unit.

Beads and ammunition are the mediums of exchange used by the intermediate men in obtaining the furs that are carried to the trading stations. Nicolai leaves at his house on the Chittystone River during his absence at Tarál beads, caps, and powder for the " Calcharnies," * who arrive and deposit an equivalent in furs, tending to show how definite is the relation between articles of commodity and prices paid for them, and also the mutual confidence amongst themselves.

Their bows and arrows are quite similar to those formerly much used by the Yukon natives, though they are perhaps a little better finished. The material for both is birch, which is subjected to a peculiar process of seasoning, which might be called tempering. A rough slab about 5 feet long is blocked out of green birch with the small ax in possession of nearly all; then the knife is used to bring it down to dimensions not exceeding an inch or inch and a half in cross-section. This rod is alternately put in the fire for a few seconds and then worked awhile with the knife until it has nearly attained its final dimensions, when it is placed where the smoke can envelop it. It may remain at this stage of the process several weeks before being again subjected to the fire and the knife. When finally tempered a bow 1 inch by $\frac{1}{2}$ inch in cross-section requires a strong arm to spring it. I have seen splendid ram-rods made of very crooked timber in the same manner.

Bows and arrows are yet largely used by them, though they are being rapidly superseded by the small-bore, double-barrel, muzzle-loading shotguns, of which there are two grades, one very inferior, the other good, with laminated steel barrels. Neither of them exceeds 5 or 6 pounds in weight. They fire out of these guns pebbles and bullets of lead or copper. The copper bullets are claimed by them to be superior to the lead ones for large game, such as moose and bear, for the reason, they say, that the copper ones will always break the bones, while the lead ones will not. The copper bullets in use on the Chittyná River are formed by hammering.

Judging from the weapons owned by these natives and from their

-----

* The term " Colcharney" or " Kolshina" is of Russian origin, and is applied by the Midnóoskies to all people not belonging to their tribe.

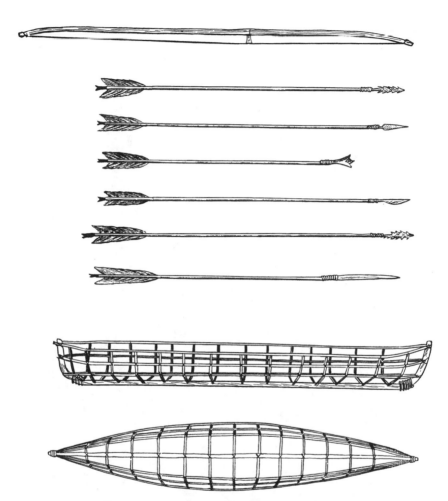

17.—Bow and arrows and Midnoosky baidarra frames.

8.—A Midnoosky cache and sled.

docile and mirthful characteristics, I should not consider them a warlike people.

In building their houses the only implements used, besides the ax and knife, is an adz made by securing to an elbowed stick with rawhide strings a flat piece of iron tempered by themselves.

They are by no means of an inventive turn, many of them obtaining their snow-shoes from the Colcharnies; nevertheless they make their toboggans and sleds, which possess the valuable qualities of lightness and durability.

As before stated, their routes of travel are chiefly on or near watercourses. When a long journey down the river is contemplated or a trip to Nuchek is decided upon, a skin boat is built; but if the distance be short, a raft made of four logs fastened with willow withes is constructed. In ascending the river with a boat only one method can be used, that of "cordelling." A party of Tatlatáns were passed above the Chitslétchina *en route* to Tarál in a baidárra for the fishing season. The skins of their boat were to be dressed at the destination and made into clothing, and the return trip was not contemplated until the ice had formed on the river, thus enabling them to sledge back. There is a trail along the river from Tarál to the mouth of Slana River, though not always on the same bank of it; in some cases it is 2 or 3 miles from the river.

To every member of a family belongs on an average three dogs, which are used for hunting moose and bear and other game, and for carrying packs. They are a source of great annoyance in the vicinity of rabbit snares unless kept at the house, usually by shoving one or both front feet through a string tied around the neck. As pack animals they are exceedingly valuable to people situated as their masters are. They do not average more than 18 to 20 inches in height, yet they can carry for short distances 30 to 33 pounds, and day after day 25 pounds. I can heartily recommend a pack train of these animals for journeys where the greatest transporting power consuming the least quantity of food is desirable. These dogs are never harnessed to the sleds, which the natives haul and push, but transport their burdens directly on the back. The men very seldom carry packs other than their arms and bedding, the work of transportation being assigned to the women, who pack themselves and manage the train of dogs. Canoe transportation in none of its forms is attempted on the Copper or any of its tributaries, nor is it probable that it ever will be, owing to the remarkably rapid current produced by the unusual fall in the river of 3,160 feet in 330 miles.

The chief amusement of these people other than eating, and the one they always resort to when hunger is satisfied, is singing. Unassisted by any musical instrument, not even any form of the *tum-tum*, nearly all join in the songs, usually led by the young men and boys. These are numerous and varied in character, those intended for courtship being much less exciting than the more epic ones. Singing is frequently indulged in while enjoying a meal, and all the bodies may be seen keeping perfect time to it. The children are taught to sing almost as soon as to talk. When dancing accompanies, its violence is in direct proportion to the stress of voice.

The spoken language is markedly accented, and seldom are more than three consecutive words uttered with the same intonation. Most dissyllabic nouns and many adjectives are accented on the last syllable. The practice of delivering orations is as frequent amongst them as among the Sioux or Cheyennes. The following limited vocabulary may serve to give a faint idea of the nature of the language. The annexed numerals of the White Mountain Apaches, as obtained from Lieut. T. B. Dugan, U. S. A.,* who was ten months on the San Carlos Reservation, shows an astonishing similarity to the same of the Atnatánas, which I trust may lead to a more thorough investigation of the matter.† On further comparison of our respective limited vocabularies a few nouns almost identical in sound and meaning were found to exist.

English.	Midnoosky.	English.	Midnoosky.
Man	Keek.	House	Hoonák.
Woman	Sekái.	Sweat-house	Sayzéll.
Child	Skunkái.	Grease	Dalkák.
Dog	Sklekáy.	To-day	Tétagin.
Salmon (small)	Slukkáy.	To-morrow	Mínta.
Salmon (large)	Sukacháy.	I	Se.
Moose	Tenáyga.	You	Nin.
Caribou	Konnái.	None, nothing, few	T'kwúlly.
Sheep	Tebáy.	Far, a long distance	Kooteshít.
Goat	S'bai.	A long time	Siyoó.
Wolf	Tekánt.	A short distance	Cuttlestée.
Fox	Nukléksy.	Good	Walláy.
Lynx	Noótëay.	Bad	Katáhwot.
Martin	Choóga.	Large	Traykchá.
Black bear	Nelláy.	Small	Tulchóne.
Brown bear	Cháhny.	Plenty	Keelán.
Rabbit	Gak.	Hot	Tebáy.
Marmot	Chiléss.	Cold	
Smooth ground	Nent.	Tired	Tazée.
Mountains	Trollái.	Hungry	Descháne.
Wood	Chitz.	To go	Hoóna.
Ice	Tin.	To come	Ah'ny.
Lake	Bin.	To sleep	Nastalá.
Water	To.	How many?	Dóna keelán?
River	Na.	Give me some water	To unto.
Sun	N̈iái.	Mount Wrangell	*Këánchilly.*
Food	Teechín.		

*I am under obligations to Lieutenant Dugan for much valuable assistance in making the report.

†Since writing this I have learned from Mr. O. T. Mason, Director of the Ethnological Department of the Smithsonian, that the relationship of the Tinneh family with the Southern Indians was discovered by Mr. Turner many years since.

English.	Midnoosky.	Apache.
One	Suskai	Daschlai.
Two	Natáyky	Nakee.
Three	Tagy	Tagy.
Four	Dinky	Dingy.
Five	Ahtzunny	Schlai.
Six	Kistán	Goostán.
Seven	Konaárry	Goosétty.
Eight	Klahínky	Saybee.
Nine	Zutlakwalo	Goostai.
Ten	Lahzún	Gooneznún.

Notwithstanding the fact that women are decidedly in the minority among the Atnatánas, polygamy is practiced to a limited extent. How far they observed the laws of consanguinity in their marriages I do not know, but that an occasional Midnoósky marries a Tatlatán is a fact, brought about possibly by that desire to avoid marriages of relations. The wives are treated with very little consideration, and are valued in proportion to their ability to pack and do general work. They and their children are always left in destitute circumstances at the death of their husband, however wealthy he may have been. This arises from the custom of distributing among the tribe at his death the property, the accumulation of which seems to be a great pride because the demonstration at the obsequies will be in proportion to the wealth of the deceased. The oldest son, however young, becomes the head of the family at the death of the father. The treatment of adopted children is not different from that of the natural heirs. Very small children are carried in a kind of birch chair or cradle, the legs hanging over, while older ones sit on the pack, with a leg passing on each side of the mother.

The social organization seems to be divided into the following classes: tyones, skillies (near relatives of a tyone), shamans or medicine-men, and vassals of varying degrees of servitude. In all assemblies seats are rigidly assigned according to rank, which is well established among them. The tyones would barely condescend to consider any of us their equals, nor did they fail to express disgust at seeing the head of our party carrying a pack or pulling on a rope.

Among the Midnoóskies the influence of the shamans is much less than with the Tatlatáns, a fact due, I suppose, to contact with the Russians. Nicolai, an influential chief, would not tolerate them, though he himself claimed to be able to perform wonderful cures; certainly many natives, far and near, believed him. His power is supposed to come from the church (Greek), of which he is an apostle. He wears on his hat a Greek cross as talisman, and has a small quantity of paper and a pencil, with which he pretends to keep a record of all matters of importance to his people. It is not strange that

with his unusually keen perceptive faculties he deceives his neigh
bors, as shown by the following: At Kheeltat's, about 350 miles from
Tarál as we traveled, was seen a native carrying a highly valued brass
cross and some hieroglyphics, both made by Nicolai, who had doubtless received a liberal allowance in furs for them. Some have such
confidence in his healing power as to send the garment of a sick
child many miles to him in order that he may sleep on it. Liebigstag, a tyone who has several shamans in his following, caused all to
absent themselves from his camp on hearing of our near approach.
Farther up the river, however, they are comparatively numerous, and
are detected by the uncombed, uncut condition of their hair. They
are non-producers, whose missions are those of priest and prophet of
the most primitive style.

The *skillies* are necessarily many, and not a few of them have
vassals at their beck and call. I have seen one fourteen or fifteen
years of age, sitting within a few feet of the river, order a man 6
feet high, a vassal, to bring him water. These menials are used for
all kinds of work, and are as completely under the control of their
masters as they possibly could be, yet I never heard of corporal
punishment being administered to them. It is but natural to suppose
that a threat of depriving them of food or shelter in their poverty-
stricken condition would be sufficient incentive to urge them to any
length of obedience.

A family is driven to a state of dependency at the death of its
head, not only on account of all property being distributed, but also
from the fact of the house being burned. The dead are put under
the ground and the site marked by a square frame, about 3 by 5 in
plan, placed above. There seems to be no special ceremony attending marriage; a man possessing a few kettles, &c., is always eligi-
ble, and when he meets his fate takes her.

TANANÁ RIVER NATIVES.

What has been said of the Atnatánas will, in a large measure,
apply to the natives of the Upper Tananá, though the frequency of
the visits of these latter to the Yukon River has had considerable
influence in modifying their customs and dress. They have almost
entirely ceased to wear nose-rings, and but few wear ornaments in
the ears. Opportunities for observing the customs of these people
were not as favorable as were those for studying the Atnatánas,
on account of the hurried manner in which we passed through the
Territory.

The natives of the Upper Tananá call that river Nabesná. For uniformity and by analogy to the term applied by Copper River natives
to themselves, I have called them Nabesnatánas. For the same
reason I have applied the term Tananatánas to all the natives of the
river. The natives of the lower part, embracing two or three small

tribes, each with a name, have for convenience been called Nukluk-tánas. The name suggests its applicability. These natives are not unlike those around Nuklúkyet. Minook, the interpreter at Fort Reliance, gave me the following names for the tribes along the Ta-naná. I record them for what they are worth. This man was never on the Tananá River, though he is considered one of the best inter-preters of the many dialects of the Tinneh language. These names are supposed to be the ones applied by the tribes to themselves. Beginning near the upper waters he says are the *Nutzotin*, includ-ing Nandell's and Tetling's following ; after them, in order, are the *Mantotin, Tolwatin, Clatchotin*, and *Huntlatin*. The termination *tin* is but another form of the word representing "people." The words *tena, tenna, tana, tinneh, tineh* have all been used to mean the same, and the word Dené, as applied to some of the people of the Hudson Bay country, is intended to represent the French phonetics for a native word meaning "people."

The Tatlatáns are not only in habitation an intermediate people between the Midnoóskies and Nabesnatánas, but also in custom and language. There are some words common to all of them, though a marked difference in the accentuation is observed between that of those north of the range and that of those south of it. A peculiar drawling tone characterizes, in a marked degree, the Nabesnatánas, in a slight degree the Tatlatáns, whilst the Midnoóskies are distin-guished by a most energetically accentuated language. These last converse with the Tatlatáns with less ease than do the latter with the Nabesnatánas, who readily communicate with the natives around Fort Reliance and Fetútlin, on the Yukon.

I estimate the entire population of the Tananá River and its tribu-taries to be between 550 and 600, though no very accurate idea can be formed of the number of a people living as they do, without visiting their settlements, very few of which are on the main river. Around Nandell's and Tetling's we counted 40 men, 32 women, and 25 chil-dren; around Kheeltat's, 28 men, 18 women, and 6 children; a total of 149. Between Kheeltat's and Toclat River there were but two camps, each containing about eight souls. Below Toclat we passed but one camp, that of Ivan, consisting of 31 men, 18 women, and 20 children. The entire number of natives seen on or near the Tananá was 232. Between Kheeltat's and Delta River, marked on the map as "head of navigation," the only indication of natives, save an occasional blazed tree, is the camping ground at the mouth of Volkmar River. Below Delta River are frequent camps, many of which are doubtless used by natives during the salmon season.

Should the Nabesnatánas descend the Tananá to its mouth for trad-ing purposes, a return could not be made until the winter time; this journey, however, is not a necessity with them, on account of their ability to obtain ammunition from Fort Reliance or Fetútlin by a portage of six days. It is not more probable that the Nukluktánas would permit them to pass through their territory than that they would those natives living between the Tananá and Kuskokwim Rivers, who must always trade through intermediate men.

That salmon do not reach the upper waters of the Tananá is rather singular, and cannot, I think, be alone attributable to the rapids along its course. The absence of salmon causes the natives to depend for sustenance on the smaller fishes previously enumerated, and large game, much of which is caught in snares. It is a custom of theirs to have long lines of fencing, so built of brush and poles that caribou or moose cannot get through it. At intervals a gap is left, in which a rope snare is placed. By this means a large part of their subsistence stores is obtained. A miner informed me that while prospecting between the Yukon and Tananá Rivers he found a "game fence" 30 miles long.

The Tananá natives have more bead work and are perhaps more skilled in its manufacture than any people seen by us in the Territory.

In general appearance and manner the natives of the Lower Tananá strongly resemble the Unakhotánas of the Yukon, especially those near Nuklúkyet. It is said by the traders of the Yukon that the natives at Fort Reliance and of Nuklúkyet understand each other, and also the Nukluktánas and Nabesnatánas, but none can understand the natives living in the vicinity of old Fort Yukon. This would seem to indicate that the Tananá River and the Yukon below the mouth of same were peopled from the upper waters of the Yukon, or else the migration was up the Tananá, thence across to Fort Reliance, leaving the most northerly part of the Yukon River to be peopled by natives from the direction of the Hudson Bay Territory. The Nabesnatánas both pack their dogs and use them in sleds, whilst the Nukluktánas, like the Yukon River natives, seldom use them otherwise than in sleds. These sleds are similar to those used on Copper River. Their dogs, however, are much larger than those of the country south of them, owing to the introduction of English breeds.

These people, like all the natives of Alaska, are natural traders, as evidenced by the number of hands through which an article will pass before being rendered unfit for use. A shirt originally belonging to the Abercrombie party was obtained at Alagánik by a Copper River native, who traded it to one of his fellows. This one wore it as far as Batzulnétas and there traded it to a native accompanying us, who carried it over Miles's Pass to Nandell's, and it was there again disposed of. In the mean time it had twice changed hands amongst the native members of our party. Had it not become worn out, it might have found its way to the Yukon. We saw at Tetling's house an ax with a Montreal brand on it, also a pair of sailor's trousers and a Thlinkit blanket, both of which doubtless came from Chilcat Inlet, the former primarily from the man-of-war stationed at Sitka.

Should the natives of the Tananá or Copper River commit outrages upon the whites who may be making their way into the interior, of such a nature as to justify the intervention of the military, many difficulties would be encountered before redress could be obtained. To stop the sale of ammunition and arms would be a sad blow to them, but a decidedly negative retaliation. To get a force into the interior marching would be necessary, and could be accomplished more easily than the party could be subsisted after its arrival at its field of action. To ascend either the Copper or Tananá by steam is out of the question. To reach Nandell's, on the north side, or Batzulnétas, on the south side, by cordelling up these rivers, would be to arrive at either place without subsistence stores. To set out from the mouth of either river when there was ice, with sleds well packed, would be to come to grief for want of food before these headwaters were reached, if an attempt were made to subsist entirely on the stores started with. This would be especially true in the case of the Tananá. The most feasible method would be to ascend the Yukon as far as Fort Reliance by steamboat, and to pack the stores across to the Tananá on the backs of men and dogs. Even after that river was reached by this method the stores would soon be exhausted unless frequent depots were made along the route and additional supplies sent forward continually. If the objective were the lower part of the Tananá River, a steamboat would solve the problem of transportation. If, however, it were the Copper River, the portage from Fort Reliance could be continued across the Alaskan Range. Once on the Copper, food in the form of salmon would be abundant, and a severe retaliation could be inflicted by patroling the river, thus preventing, if possible, the natives from taking fish during the summer. By this means a large number of them would perish the following winter.

From extensive observation and from conversation with men who have traveled extensively in the Territory, I am of the opinion that pack animals other than dogs or reindeer are not practicable anywhere in the interior save in an occasional locality, and then for a short distance, not exceeding a few miles. That other than these would die during the winter, unless special provision were made, there can be no doubt. The footing in many places would render an ordinary mule pack train of as little or less value than a flotilla of small boats. Grass in these high latitudes has given place to a deep bed of moss and lichens, which it is hardly probable would subsist horses, mules, or oxen. Occasionally small sections of the Territory are seen where the growth of grass is luxuriant, yet such an occurrence is generally accompanied by the sight of marshes. It is a significant fact that the burning of the moss gives rise to a hardy growth of grass, which practice may in the future be advantageously used.

In view of the above considerations, special care should be taken in selecting a force to be sent into this country. Each man should be chosen for his obedience, strength, endurance, and ability to live in a country where food is difficult to obtain; in other words, each should be soldier, hunter, packer, and his own commissary. I know of no class of men so capable of fulfilling these conditions as mineral prospectors, whose occupation frequently requires the exercise of such accomplishments.

Strategically considered there are no people within the boundaries of the United States so favorably situated as the above-mentioned tribes of the Tinneh family. Gifted by nature with the skill and cunning of their southern relations, and inhabiting a much more inaccessible and foodless country, depredations and other crimes could be committed with correspondingly greater impunity.

NATIVES OF THE KÓYUKUK RIVER.

Notwithstanding the vast extent of country occupied by these people, they differ so little from each other that the term Koyukuns, previously used, may with propriety be applied to all of them . They belong to the Tinneh family, and possibly the term Koyuktána, or "Koyukuk-Khotana" would, for uniformity, be more properly applied.

The river on which they live possesses a moderate current, is free from falls or rapids, hence offers a ready and easy way for communication; yet I doubt whether the natives on its upper waters will descend it to its mouth so long as they can trade at Nuklúkyet or meet the fur traders at Konoótena village.

Their most northern settlement, which is in approximate latitude 66° 44′, longitude 150° 47′, is on the Nohoolchintna near its mouth, while the most southern one is near the junction of the river with the Yukon, more than 500 miles below. All of these people readily converse with the Unakhotánas at Nuklúkyet and Nuláto, though some words are entirely different from those used at the nearest points on the Yukon to represent the same idea.

In appearance they differ so little from their Yukon relations that a description of them seems hardly necessary. They are on record, according to all persons who have written of them, as being warlike people, due perhaps to their participation in the Nuláto massacre, previously mentioned. Those living on the upper part of the river are too poverty-stricken and miserable to attempt anything that would not assist them in obtaining food or clothing. They report that a severe epidemic carried away many of their number in the winter of 1882–'83. At the only villages above Batzakákat, viz, Konootená and Nohoolchíntna, are eleven men, four of whom, together with one woman and one child, are deaf-mutes. We did not see all of the inhabitants of the last-named village, so it is possible there may be others similarly afflicted.

The total number of Koyukuns, estimating the settlements on the Hussliakátna and Cawtaskákat as containing fourteen and ten, respectively, is 276. This is a more accurate census than can usually be made of the natives. Besides these there was an Innuit family of five living temporarily on the river. To show how the Kóyukuk is populated, I cite the following: Between Red Shirt's village and the extreme northern settlement, a distance by the river of 363 miles, were thirteen settlements, temporary and permanent, with inhabitants numbering 164; between Red Shirt's village and the mouth of the river were five settlements, containing 65 souls; while at his village alone were 45. Of this population it is noticed that 66 are men, 79 women, and 129 children, a fact that shows that the division as to sex is very different from that usually found among uncivilized people who struggle so hard for existence.

The principal subsistence of these people is fish, which includes several varieties besides the salmons, chief among which in point of numbers is the *dog salmon*. They bemoan most bitterly the scarcity of game, and at several settlements they endeavored to purchase a young caribou skin, part of my bed, to use in making winter clothing. The existence of a people living under such adverse circumstances as do those of the upper part of the river cannot be of long duration. Before the 12th of August they had had a warning of winter in the form of a snow squall.

Many of the Koyukuns are armed with old-fashioned rim-fire Winchester magazine rifles, caliber .44, which have been obtained, through the Eskimos, from whaling vessels. While possessing this gun, it is seldom that it can be utilized for want of cartridges. Besides these they have shot-guns, usually the single-barrel muzzle-loader, and bows and arrows.

They make portages over the mountains to the north from Fickett, Allenkákat, and Dakliakákat Rivers, presumably to the Colville and Kówuk, or Holöotána River, as the Koyukuns call it. They also portage to the Tozikákat and descend it to the Yukon, or else use the trail we followed from the Yukon. Those lower down pass to the headwaters of the Kotzebue Sound, where they exchange commodities with the Eskimos. Natives from Red Shirt's village have occasionally gone as far as Saint Michael's to trade. Now that Nuláto is abandoned, such journeys will be almost a necessity if they desire to trade during the winter season.

What may be said with respect to the education of the Yukon natives will equally apply to these.

I know of no place in the possession of the United States where charity could with more justice be dispensed than among these people and those of the Lower Yukon. If the Government desires that this people should continue to exist, some provision for them should soon be made. Fish food is sufficiently abundant to support them, but the prospects of obtaining clothing material are rapidly growing darker. It is a mistaken idea, that of supposing the interior of Alaska possessed of much large game. To show the scarcity of such, I will say that during our entire travel from latitude 60° 20' to 50 miles within the Arctic Circle, thence to Saint Michael's, over a route covering 18° of longitude, we did not see a single moose or caribou, and but one bear, a small black one. During the greater part of the winter of 1884–'85 Messrs. Mayo and La Due, who wintered at Fort Reliance, had rabbits only for meat, notwithstanding repeated efforts were made by themselves and their Indian hunters to obtain large game.

THE NATIVES OF THE YUKON.

The natives of the Yukon River, from the mouth of the Tananá to the sea, have been described by Dall and others, and the term " Ingalik " has been applied to those living between Nuláto and that part of the country occupied by the Innuits, or Eskimos. This word is of Eskimo origin, and was originally used by them to represent all the inland people. The name given by the Ingaliks to themselves, however, is Kaiyu-Khotana, which means people of the lowlands (Dall). Their appearance shows them to be the Tinneh family, modified by a liberal infusion of Eskimo blood.

Their continued intercourse with Russians and whites for fifty years has had its effect in altering their customs, though it is not evident that the association has been beneficial to them. With the introduction of fire-arms was begun an extermination of the once numerous herds of caribou, which supplied clothing and a liberal part of their food. The scarcity of these animals now causes a greater dependence on the traders for clothing and at the same time deprives them of a possible source of revenue from the sale of its meat and sinew. They must now depend almost solely on fish and berries to continue their existence as a people.

Beginning at Nuklúkyet and descending the Yukon, the increase of poverty and squalor is very noticeable. A marked loss of self-respect is also apparent. Their poverty-stricken, humiliated condition is taken advantage of by the traders, who demand from them much greater prices for the usual commodities than are obtained from the bolder and more independent natives who assemble at the trading stations farther up the river. Had these people a sale for the thousands of excellent salmon that yearly ascend their rivers their future would not be so dark as it now necessarily is. Between Nuklúkyet and Yakutskalítnik I saw many natives who barely had sufficient material to hide their nakedness, and furthermore their prospects of obtaining winter clothing were indeed meager. The destruction of the large game has been very rapid, and whether or not these natives will survive the resulting destitution without governmental interposition is doubtful.

The Iṅgaliks constitute the most numerous tribe of the Tinneh family in the Territory of Alaska, and may be estimated to number 1,300.

I have used Dall's designation for the natives living between the mouth of the Tananá and Nuláto, Mnakho-tana, which includes the inhabitants of the two last-named places. They number about 550 souls. The blending of these natives with the Iṅgaliks is so uniform that no exact line can be drawn separating the two. Both are called by themselves Yukoni-khotánas, which means people of the Yukon River country.

Neither these nor the In'galiks are governed by the tyone system. A stronger influence is probably exerted by the shamans, who include in their numbers both sexes. It will require a long time to eradicate the much-abused faith imposed in them by their parishioners. Minook, a sensible Indian, who speaks English, was, to judge from his conversation, much opposed to shamanism. His child at Nuklúkyet having become seriously ill with "summer complaint," he applied to me for medicine, which I gave. Unwilling to await results, and probably having become convinced that the child was too sick for white man's medicine, the shaman was called about midnight to begin his incantations. These were continued every few nights until the child died. The shaman in attendance was a smart, fine-looking young man, reputed to possess great powers. I give below his method, which, though homeopathic as far as relates to the child, was decidedly allopathic as to himself. A piece of canvas was spread on the ground, around which all the natives at the village sat singing an intermittent, spirited chant or dirge. On the canvas was the shaman, covered with a blanket, with which several Indians were trying to conceal and keep him on the canvas, while he was groaning, yelling, and indulging in all sorts of contortions, all the while keeping time with his noises and kicks to the spasmodic singing of the surrounding group. At one corner of the canvas Minook, with his child in his arms, was sitting. After writhing and groaning under the blanket for an hour or more, the shaman thrust his feet into Minook's lap, under the wraps of the child. He lay in that position for some time, when he broke away with the disease of the child in his possession. Then began a terrible struggle with the disease in order to drive it back into the keeping of the evil spirit. During this contest he tore his shirt from his body, floundered to the top of the blanket, and seemed to suffer the most excruciating pains. At the end of about two hours, when his exertions had become less violent, one of the natives seized him, drew his head into his lap, blew into one ear, then into the other, and then pressed hard on the top of his head. The shaman remained in a stupor until a second Indian jumped up and gave him another pressure on the head, which completed the process of resuscitation and enabled him to immediately arise and join in the general conversation. At another time he made a medicine while under the blanket and fastened it around the child's neck, before coming from under his cover.

The result of the teachings and example of Mr. Simms, a deceased missionary of the Church of England, is plainly noticeable, and as valuable to the traders as to the natives, all of whom express a warm feeling for his memory. There are now, besides the hundreds of Indian children along the Lower Yukon, the Lower Kuskokwim, and the coast north and south of Saint Michael's, twelve or fifteen half-breed children of traders living at present on the Yukon, who are very desirous that their offspring should be educated, and who affirm that the Indian parents in a large measure wish the same advantages for theirs. The only place of instruction available is the Mission, 217 miles from the coast, where the preceptor is a half-breed Russian priest, incapable of teaching English.

The question of an industrial education, the system of instruction now supposed to be best for Indian children, for the Yukon River natives, is certainly a subject for consideration. The question naturally suggests itself, what industry can be taught children living in such an inhospitable climate as theirs, where winter begins the first of September and ends the middle of May, when the ice goes out of the river? The primary object of the education should be to teach them more feasible methods of living. If it be proved that their country is capable of producing the hardy vegetables and grain, or that it is rich in mineral resources, then their education will find fields for its application. If, however, it continue in the future what it has been to them in the past, valuable only for its fish and game, instruction of any kind would be of doubtful value. For now, after generations of experience, do they not better understand securing their fish and animal food than white men can teach them? Of the former they obtain all they desire, while of the latter they secure yearly all that can be and more than should be taken. Their houses are quite in keeping with their mode of living, and good enough for their present surroundings; why change them? Without the further development of their country, or financial assistance, I cannot see that the benefits of an industrial education would in any manner be for their welfare. The education of the natives in Southern Alaska, whereby they are better prepared for several industries which are established in or near their homes, is quite a different affair. In their own country there is at present no employment open to the Yukon natives and their neighbors save the securing of food and the trapping of a few fur-bearing animals. The policy of educating them and sending them to another part of our country for employment would be an extremely questionable one, as would be that of educating them elsewhere and sending them back to their people. With plenty of food and warm clothes there is no reason why these people, who have for generations inhabited the Yukon, should not continue to so do; but with food consisting of fish only, and a scarcity of clothing material brought about by an improvident destruction of large game, their existence from a sociological point of view is not long.

If tribes of Indians living in the West and Southwest of the United States, where the climate is genial as compared to that of the interior of Alaska, and where food products are comparatively easily obtainable, receive, as a matter of right or policy, support from the Government in part or whole, certainly these people, nearly destitute of clothing, should at least have assistance in that direction.

That their moral and spiritual welfare could be much improved by schools, and that their ideas respecting sanitary laws could be vantageously modified, is not to be questioned; yet by all means let such changes be accompanied with presents of wearing apparel. The traders informed me that there has already been much suffering during the winters from want of proper clothing.

The entire number of souls on the Yukon above Nuklúkyet is estimated at five to six hundred; but these have as yet not seriously suffered for want of skins for clothing material. In general appearance they resemble the Nabesnatánas.

ESKIMOS, OR INNUITS.

It is not within the scope of this report to enter into a description of the customs and manner of living of the Eskimos of Alaska, for the reason that more or less has been written about them from the time of the discovery of Stewart Island, on which Saint Michael's is situated, until the present time. For their description, numbers, and location I would refer the reader to the report of Mr. Ivan Petroff, special agent of the census, which is as reliable as any publication on the subject. I will say, however, that any attempt at an accurate census would require more time than was allotted to Mr. Petroff.

Captain Healy, commanding the *Corwin*, whose observations in Northern Alaska have extended over a period of fifteen years, estimates the number of Eskimos from Saint Michael's along the coast to Point Barrow at 3,000, and the number in the interior between these two points at 2,000. The number between Saint Michael's and Cook's Inlet, including the interior, according to Mr. Petroff, is about 9,800.

The same general characteristics may be seen among all the Alaskan Eskimos. A single glance at the accompanying photograph is sufficient to at once distinguish the subjects of it from the Indians of the interior.

The picture fairly represents the type. The central figure is that of a native employed by us on the Kóyukuk, and who served as our pilot from the village at the mouth of that river to Saint Michael's. In general they live near the coast, where food is more easily obtainable, though in the interior a few were met on the Upper Kóyukuk at probably the greatest distance from salt water that they are ever found. The few natives that people the Upper Kówuk and Nówatak are the same family.

Besides the foregoing, the principal natives are the Aleuts, who live on the Aleutian Islands, and the Kolóshes, or Thlinkets, who occupy Southeastern Alaska from near the mouth of Copper River to the southernmost limit of the Territory.

PART V.

OBSERVATIONS.

SOME OF THE ANIMALS OF ALASKA.
GEOLOGICAL OBSERVATIONS.
VOLCANIC ACTION.
GLACIAL AND DILUVIAL DEPOSITS.
MINERALS.

147

SOME OF THE ANIMALS OF ALASKA.

In mentioning the animals of Alaska I will begin with those used by the natives for food. While we did not see all of the forms named in the following brief descriptions in their wild states, their pelts or flesh, sometimes both, were at some time of the journey found either in the possession of the natives or the traders of the Yukon, and carefully examined. To the latter practically all the furs of the Yukon shed are carried and through them transferred to Saint Michael's, whence they are transported to San Francisco.

Of the ruminants I mention first the Cervidæ family, in which the moose, *Alces machlis*, is given precedence on account of its importance as a food and clothing producing animal. It is almost identical with that found in Northern Maine and formerly in Northern Minnesota, and is the animal which the natives largely depend upon for fat in certain parts of the Territory. It is claimed that they seek the islands of the rivers to bring forth the young, where they have greater immunity from wolves and mosquitoes than is offered on the hills and mountains. If this be true, it is to me but another proof of the scarcity of the animal in the Territory, for our courses along the rivers were necessarily among the islands, on which we frequently landed, to find nothing more than an occasional track. The natives, like most hunters, value the nose as the choicest part of the moose, and I doubt if any one who has tried it will question their taste.

Three forms of the *Rangifer tarandus* are supposed to be known to the Territory—the barren-ground caribou, the woodland caribou, and the reindeer—the former being confined to Northern Alaska. The two latter-named species, if both exist, south of the Yukon, are, to the best of my knowledge, called by the natives by the same name, *honnai*. The average *honnai* when dressed will weigh from 200 to 250 pounds. Its horns seem to partake both of the nature of those of common deer and of the moose, the ends of some branches being flattened, while others are rounded. None of these animals are spotted, as are the reindeer of the Asiatic side, but all become very light in color during the winter. On the Copper and Tananá Rivers these animals, as well as the moose, are hunted when the snow is deep and hard, with the aid of dogs, when they are brought to bay and killed at short distances. A native has, indeed, been known to run down a moose and kill him with a knife, but this is rare. They

149

are also snared, as previously described. There is a species of deer, quite numerous, inhabiting Southern Alaska and the Archipelago, but it does not find its way far into the interior. It is probably the *Cariacus columbianus*, or Columbia black-tailed deer, somewhat changed by the condition of his surroundings. These constitute a large portion of the meat ration of Sitka and Juneau. I have the skin of one of these animals now in my possession, which is about the same shade of blue as the fur seal, though this color is not the rule.

Of the Bovidæ family there are two recognized species, the *Mazama montana*, or the small-horned goat of the Rocky Mountains, white in color. This animal has black horns, with little curvature, and is found on the Copper River and the Upper Yukon. The *Ovis montana dalli* is a new geographical race of the mountain sheep or big-horn. It has been described as follows by Mr. E. W. Nelson, formerly of the United States Signal Corps:

> This form can be recognized at once by the nearly uniform dirty-white color, the light-colored rump, as seen in typical *Montana*, being entirely uniform with the rest of the body in *Dalli*. The dinginess of the white over the entire body and limbs appears to be almost entirely due to the ends of the hairs being commonly tipped with a dull rusty speck. On close examination this tipping of the hairs makes the fur look as though it had been slightly singed. This form also has smaller horns than its southern relatives, but how the two compare in general size and weight I am unable to say. I name this form in honor of Mr. W. H. Dall, whose scientific work in Alaska is so well known.

Whether the big-horn mountain sheep, *Ovis canadensis*, exists in Alaska I am unable to say, but I desire to add also a new geographical race of the same. The animal in question is called by the natives *tebáy*, and this name I leave unchanged until a specimen will have been carried out of the Territory. We killed several of these animals, one of which, a ram, had horns 20 inches long and nearly straight. Their structure was similar to that of the big-horn, but the curvature was very slight. This ram was killed on a very high point, such a place as is usually sought by them, and in its fall was sadly mangled. The head of the *tebáy* is much like that of a Southdown sheep, the muzzle much less pointed than in Nelson's big-horn. The hair is of a uniform white, in fact, nearly equal to his snow surroundings in color, and is nearly as easily broken as that of the antelope. Next to the skin is a very fine short wool, which is very strong. In size the *tebáy* is probably an equal of its relative, the big-horn. I saw a spoon made from the horn of one that measured 26 inches in length and 5 inches across the bowl. We were informed that some had much larger horns than the one that furnished material for this spoon. This, like most statements of natives, is questionable. The large ram and one other were killed on the most northerly tributary of the Chittystone River. The natives informed us that small *tebáy* could be killed a few miles below the junction of the Chittystone, a fact we doubted, and hence chose to allow them the use of our carbines. They passed the night on the mountains north of the Chittyná River, and returned with four small ones that would weigh when dressed probably 65 pounds. The heads were left on the mountains, but the bodies brought in seemed identical with those obtained on the Chittystone River. Why only small ones should be found at this place in the latter part of April I cannot say; yet the mountains here were not so high as farther to the east, where the large ones had been killed. The last of these animals seen or heard of by us were near the headwaters of Copper River, on the divide between it and the Tananá River.

As a food-producing animal in the interior of the Territory, the rabbit takes rank next. Had there been none of these our prospects would have been more gloomy than can well be described. For days and weeks almost our sole dependence was on these little animals, and during a season when they did not possess a particle of fat. They are probably the *northern varying* hare, possibly a little different from those found in New England. In size they are probably intermediate between the "rabbit" of the Middle States and the "jack rabbit" of the plains of Northern United States. The ears are very long and the tips of them is the only portion of the animal that is not covered with snow-white fur during the winter. During the deep snow period their only food is from the trees, many of which are barked all around near the ground by them. During this period groves of small cottonwoods or birches are favorite resorts for them and can be relied on to furnish a meal, providing the hunter is skilled in quietly passing through timber. The polar hare, *Lepus timidus*, is much larger than the "jack rabbit" of the plains, and is generally confined to the far north of the Territory. The pelts of both these varieties of hares are largely used for clothing and blankets.

The beaver is quite universally distributed throughout the Territory, and is valuable as a food as well as for its pelt. Its habits are not unlike those practiced by the same animal farther south.

The Felicidæ or cat family claims the Canada lynx as probably the only variety inhabiting Alaska. This is the animal known in Montana as the "bob-tail cat," much larger, however, and while prized for its fur is also valued for its meat, which is by no means unpalatable, as many would suppose.

In the Canidæ family there are four varieties of foxes and two of wolves. The former are the arctic, red, cross, and silver or black foxes, valued for the pelts in the inverse order of the naming. The arctic fox, *Vulpes lagopus*, found specially in the most northern districts, is white in winter and of a bluish tint in summer. I have never heard of them south of the Alaskan Mountains. The other varieties are more generally distributed, though the trading station at Fort Reliance receives annually about 75 pelts of black or silver foxes, *Fulvus argentatus* variety, which is more than all the other stations of the Yukon obtain. The wolves are the gray and the black, both large and quite scarce. Their pelts are specially valued by the natives for trimming other furs, and, like the wolverine skins, are in such demand that but few leave the Territory, the natives being willing to give a greater equivalent in other furs than would justify their shipment by the traders.

The bear family is represented by three varieties in the interior, the black, the brown, and the grizzly, besides the white bear of the coast and northern islands. There were several hunting parties landed from the *Corwin* on Hall's Island, north of the Aleutian group, on her return, and on one of the hunts Mr. Townsend, of the Smithsonian, killed one of the last-named animals. The black bear is most frequently met, though thee xperience of others as well as ourselves is that it is possible to see but few of any description.

Of the weazel family I mention first the North American otter, valuable only for its fur, and generally known as the land-otter. The wolverine, about equal in value to the land-otter, is a rather rare animal, possessing a long, coarse fur, more highly appreciated by the natives than by more civilized people. The common mink is the most numerous of the fur-bearing animals of the interior, and more abundant on the lower Yukon than elsewhere. Next to it in numbers is the American marten, or sable, considered the unit of exchange in the dealings between the traders and the natives, and for which one dollar in merchandise, at Alaska prices, is given.

I should not fail to mention the musk-rat, a variety of the mouse family, which more than once helped serve us as a meal. In size they are about one-half that of the same animal of the Middle States. Their skins are much used for blankets and parkies.

Of the squirrel family but two varieties were seen, the little marmot, *Arctomys priunosus*, which forms such an important factor in clothing the natives, and a very small gray squirrel of a reddish tinge, generally found in spruce timber.

The porcupine has been previously mentioned.

For description of the sea animals the reader is referred to a report on the seal fisheries by Mr. H. W. Elliott, of the Smithsonian. The subject of fisheries has not been touched in this report, though a great deal could be said in reference to it, notwithstanding what has already been written. There is practically no limit to the quantity of salmon that can be taken in the limits of the Territory, including the coast waters and the rivers. At present the extreme low prices are discouraging to the establishments already in operation. Salmon in the San Francisco market is worth little more than one-third the amount paid for them a few years since. The increase in the cod fisheries has been indeed wonderful, and this notwithstanding little or no efforts have been made to survey the cod banks. This industry may be said to have had its origin in 1880, since which time the statistics are quite interesting. The manufacture of oil from herring by the Northwest Fur and Trading Company is an industry of considerable proportions, and capable of much greater developments should the markets demand. I have previously reported to the Government on this establishment. When the Western country will have become as thickly populated as the most populous States the fish of Alaska will be of untold value in supporting its inhabitants.

GEOLOGICAL OBSERVATIONS.

VOLCANIC ACTION.

If we inquire when those mighty masses of bold and picturesque rock, covering hundreds of square miles, were upheaved, we must look for answer to the same causes that are the foundations of the theories respecting the ranges in the western part of the United States. It is reasonably supposed that the Rocky Mountain Range in early geological history constituted the land of the western part of our country, and that the face of the earth to its west, now represented by mountain ranges and valleys, was then water.

During the Paleozoic and a great portion of the Mesozoic eras this huge chain was subjected to erosions, resulting in deposits which were upheaved in the rudimentary Sierra Nevada and Cascade Ranges, followed much later by the upheaval of the Coast Range. Volcanic action and erosion have served to present them as we see them to-day. If this theory be true, it is possible that the same conditions were coexistent in Alaska, as the ranges now help to attest. The Rocky Mountains extend to the Arctic Ocean by following a course nearly parallel with that portion of the Yukon River between old Fort Selkirk and Fort Yukon, while to the south of the Yukon are the Alaskan Range, which attains its loftiest elevations in the *sickle* of Copper River, and the Saint Elias Range, extending around Prince William's Sound to beyond Cook's Inlet, its northerly limit being the Chittyná River. Both these ranges now have active volcanoes, as did the Cascade and Coast Ranges very recently. In fact, it has been claimed by some who have visited Mount Hood that sulphurous gases are yet escaping from near its summit, while Mount Saint Helen's has been described by more than one eye-witness as an active volcano.

Notwithstanding the appearance of a new volcano, Bogoslov, in 1883, just north of Oonalaska Island, it is supposed that volcanic action is less than existed in the Territory during its earliest occupation. This supposition is a doubtful one, owing to the fact that the records relative to the matter date back only to the latter part of the seventeenth century. More than fifty peaks are known to have at times been seen in action, and some of these that are now quiet may again become active from the old craters, as our limited records have shown, or else may form new cones, as in the case of Bogoslov, about which several persons have recently written. During our visit to that volcano it was emitting vapors and sulphurous gases in such quantities as to nearly conceal its upper portion. A few hundred yards distant was the old Bogoslov, quietly resting, as though satisfied with her offspring. Mount Wrangell, elevation 17,500 feet, was, during our stay in the Copper River Valley, continually sending up a light vapor, apparently uniform in volume, while during a great portion of the winter of 1884–'85 it was, according to the only eye-witness other than natives, John Bremner, emitting grand volumes of smoke and fire, such as to present a weird and sublime picture. He claims that the fire shot above the crater a distance that appeared three times greater than the height of the mountain. Whether all the prominent peaks in this vicinity possess extinct craters could not be determined, though Mount Drum readily showed that it was an extinct volcano.

South of the Tananá River and north of the Kuskokwim is an extension of the Alaskan Range containing some peaks several thousand feet higher than exist where we crossed the range; yet no volcanic action exists.

North of the Yukon to the Arctic the ranges are comparatively low; the highest are Endicott Mountains, between the Kóyukuk and Kówuk Rivers, which doubtless contain the headwaters of the Colville River. I am disposed to think that no volcanic activity has ever been witnessed in Alaska in a higher latitude than is Mount Wrangell (approximately 62° 25′ N.), notwithstanding the reports relative to the peaks south of the Tananá, previously alluded to.

GLACIAL AND DILUVIAL DEPOSITS.

Diluvium is found everywhere, and the Territory of Alaska is a striking picture of that deposited by ice rivers or glaciers as well as mountain torrents. The existence of rolled pebbles and bowlders, sometimes in huge quantities in the high banks of streams, sometimes on the tops and declivities of mountains as well as in the valleys between, their entire dissimilarity from the rocks of the country in which they lie, are geological characteristics specially noticeable in the Copper River shed.

In the study of the action of water in its relation to geological changes American students have always found an ample field at home. Not so, however, with respect to glacial actions, for we find our most exhaustive treatise on this subject confined almost exclusively to the Alps glaciers. Let our specialists in the future seek fields in our own province, where the system is probably more extensive than in any other country south of the Arctic Circle. I refer to that portion of the Territory from Chilcat Inlet up to Cook's Inlet, and especially to that portion drained by the Copper River.

How far glacial action has been concerned in the determination of the topography will long be a subject for study. My observations are such as to cause a belief in an ice sheet that at one time extended from the Alaskan Mountains to the coast (as to how much farther from the north it came I have nothing to say). It may at first be considered at variance with the theory of contemporary upheaval of this part of the Territory with the ranges of the western part of the United States; an examination, however, of the true condition of affairs will reconcile this. Long after the upheaval followed the glacial period, producing the ice-sea, which by its steady motion to the south has largely assisted in giving the country its present configuration.

From Yakutat Bay to the mouth of Copper River is an unbroken face of ice for a distance of 50 miles. How far this extends to the interior through the gorges of the coast range is unknown, though it may be safe to consider the distance equal to that of the glaciers of Copper River from its mouth. These latter may be considered an extension of the ice fronting the coast, which the Copper River formerly flowed under. There is every reason to believe that Miles's and Childs' Glaciers at one time were one and the same, an opinion that is in some way strengthened by the tradition of the natives. The most southerly point of the former on the left bank is 1 mile or less from the most northerly point of the latter on the right bank, while in the river-bed between are well-worn bowlders, 8 to 12 feet in diameter, and on the left bank, below Miles's Glacier and opposite Childs' Glacier, is an enormous glacial drift, now covered with vegetation. Where it joins to Miles's it is impossible to distinguish the drift from the glacier. The flow of these is now doubtless from east to west for those on the left bank, and from west to east for those on the right bank; yet this is probably not the general course the ice masses had when they were much larger than at present. They are but a residuum of the once extensive ice fields now discharging along the paths of least resistance. Had not the climate here been moist and favorable for glacier-making, the present site would have been occupied by only drift or moraine, as is the case farther north, above the Chittyná, on the east bank of the Copper River, where for many miles are terraces, large and small, the deposits of ancient glaciers. The smaller ones are so regularly formed as to leave the impression that they were the fronts of old fortifications. In Blake's Stickeen River he makes mention of the scarcity of well-defined terraces, while Dall failed to observe any in the vicinity of Sitka and the Alaska Peninsula. The source of both the Copper and Chittyná Rivers are glaciers, though indeed small when compared to the ones above mentioned.

I can only account for the remarkable width of the bed of the Copper by the supposition that it was excavated by the power of gigantic ice masses and the eroding effects of the torrent waters from it. The volume of water in proportion to the width of bed is less than in any river within my knowledge, while the banks, as a rule, are steep and

high.   By an examination of the map it will be seen that the Alaskan Mountains form an arc convex to the northward; hence the lines
of least resistance of ice masses in moving from these mountains to
the southward tended to intersect in the present Copper Valley.
The power obtained by the enormous flow from all sides produced
the remarkable excavations cited above.

I earnestly hope that glacial action in this district will receive
early attention at the hands of competent men.   A simple inspection
of the map of Alaska by a student of nature will show that this spot
was the scene of most powerful action, the traces of which are correspondingly clearly preserved.

North of the Alaskan Mountains I failed to see any of these remarkable glacial phenomena, though from reports of miners they
may be found on the White River.

MINERALS.

The minerals of Copper River have long been a source of specula-
tion, owing to pieces of pure copper, knives and bullets of the same
metal, having been brought down to the coast by the natives.   Some
of the specimens are supposed to be associated with native silver,
and in fact I had heard of some brought down which was reported
to have assayed in Boston $80 per ton in silver and 60 per cent. of
copper.   Nicolai's house is supposed to be in the heart of the mineral
region, and by him we were shown the locality of a vein which at
that season of the year, April, was above the snow line.   He gave
us, however, some specimens which proved to be bornite, a sulphuret
of copper and iron.   He said the pure copper was on the Chittyto
River, between his house and the central branch of the Chittyná, as
well as on the other tributaries of the same.   He had bullets of pure
copper in his possession, obtained, he said, from the natives over the
mountains, though his supply consisted of three or four.   We found
specimens of bornite also in the hands of the natives at Nandell's,
just north of the range.   I do not believe that the natives guard as
a secret treasure the copper or other mineral beds, but think that
they would willingly reveal to the white man their knowledge in the
matter.

The two prospectors of my party found with difficulty *color* at the
mouth of Copper River, but were not at all pleased with the prospects farther up.

In ascending the Copper River it was observed that the banks,
especially the east one, about 20 miles below Tarál, were a green horn-
blendic rock, intersected by small mineral-bearing quartz veins.
These gave way to a green basalt near the southern extremity of
Wood's Cañon, which had at its northern end a fine quality of
slate that split easily into laminæ transversely to its bed.   Parts of
the bluff showed more than one distinct cleavage.

A few miles from the mouth of the Chittyná it cuts through bluffs of beautiful greenstone, intersected by white veins, which appeared to be limestone. The pebbles and bowlders of this river-bed are much discolored by copper stains, but not to such a remarkable degree as those of its tributary, the Chittystone. The mountains around the headwaters of the latter are sandstone and felspathic granite.

A feature of some of the high banks of the Upper Copper are the strata of bowlders, many feet below the surface, and separated by a distance of 6 to 8 feet. These banks are specially remembered on account of an incident occurring at the foot of one which disabled one of my native employés. As the frost leaves the face of the banks the pebbles and bowlders become loose and start down the steep bank to the river. To pass them without injury it is necessary to be a skillful dodger. A very strong native was struck in the head by one, which sent him to the ground with a profusion of blood from the nose, disabling him for further work.

On the east bank of the Copper, about 8 miles above Gakoná River, is a deposit of fragmentary porphyritic rock 8 feet below the surface and 50 feet above the water line. On the Alaskan Mountains, not far from Lake Suslóta, is a bed of pebbles and bowlders immediately under the vegetation.

The banks of the Upper Tananá, where there is rock, are generally composed of a yellowish granite, fast undergoing disintegration, as evidenced by the innumerable particles of mica suspended in the river and the ever-shifting quicksands. On the lower river the rocky banks are more basaltic in appearance. There has been little or no attempt at prospecting on this river. Our party tried for color a number of times without success.

There have been, within the last few years, a number of miners on the Upper Yukon and its tributaries, in search of gold. So far their success has been but partial; the best result that has come within my knowledge was an equivalent of $1,100 in gold and platinum, taken from a bar in the river by two men in one season. Gold-bearing quartz of a very low grade has been found in a few places, but its value would hardly justify the working of it.

On the northern bank of the Kóyukuk are indications of coalbeds, as shown on the map. The geological formation of the country drained by this river is in appearance very similar to that of the Yukon from Yakutskalítnik up, so that what may be written with respect to the geology of the Yukon will in a large measure apply to it.

There are two mines in Alaska that promise well, viz, the galena mines near Golovína Bay, Norton Sound, and the gold-quartz mines of Douglas Island. In a recent report to the commanding general, Department of Columbia, I stated that if the cost of working the latter mine were twice that claimed, and the return of metal one-half the amount claimed, the property would be a most valuable one.

In these few brief observations I do not pretend to enumerate all the claims to mineral wealth of the Territory. The coal measures in different parts will certainly deserve consideration, and may in the future prove of great value.

The various reports relative to the mineral wealth of Alaska, some of which appear over the names of Territorial officials, are decidedly sensational and unreliable. There may be, and probably is, great mineral wealth in the interior, but as yet its location is unknown. From the nature of the country and shortness of the seasons, many years will be required to thoroughly ascertain the localities of valuable mineral veins. It is not my intention to discourage immigration to the Territory, yet I would gladly warn all who contemplate it to regard with suspicion many of the current articles relative to the mineral wealth.

PART VI.

METEOROLOGY.

METEOROLOGY.

SIR: In submitting the following meteorological report I cannot but regret that the information which it contains is in so many respects incomplete.

You always led our small party and participated equally in the hardships and sufferings of the expedition, sometimes dividing your small share of rotten fish or scraps of tallow with those who needed it perhaps less than you did. Hence it is not to you that I enumerate some of the trying circumstances under which the observations were taken, but to those who may look through these pages and perhaps wonder why so much valuable data are lacking.

In the first place, geographical and physical, rather than meteorological, knowledge was the object of the expedition. In the second place, our supplies having been necessarily abandoned at the mouth of Copper River in March, we were reduced to the absolute necessity of reaching the coast on Bering Sea or some provisioned trading-post on the Yukon River before winter set in, or of taking the chances of surviving a winter in that northern and inhospitable region without food, clothing, or supplies of any kind. Under these conditions nearly everything was sacrificed to rapid locomotion, traveling till exhausted, without regard to day or night, being a frequent necessity.

The absence of observations between March 20 and April 8, the time occupied in traveling from Núchek to Tarál, will be accounted for by the fact that we were in an almost continuous storm of rain, sleet, or snow, accompanied by a cold, cutting wind, and were often wading in slush to our knees. We had no tentage, no protection from the raging elements except such as was furnished by our saturated clothing and wet blankets. Cold, hungry, and exhausted, we struggled on over that desolate and barren waste, making every exertion possible to get into the interior of the country and out of reach of the everlasting storms of the coast region. Under these conditions instrumental observations were utterly impossible.

At Tarál we learned that the copper deposits, from which Copper River is supposed to derive its name, were situated on its eastern tributary, the Chittyná. You decided to visit these deposits, and, as our time was limited, it was necessary that we make long and rapid marches and live on the country. Accordingly everything not absolutely needed was *cached* at this place, and with comparatively light packs on our backs we started on the march. The trip required about a month, and on our return to the Copper River regular meteoro-

logical observations were begun and continued with as much uniformity as was possible under existing circumstances. They were
taken before leaving camp in the morning, generally about sunrise,
and upon going into camp at night, from about 7 p. m. to midnight.
During the day the instruments were rolled up in my blanket, which
was securely bound in a compact bundle for convenient handling and
packing. In this manner the observations were taken till our arrival
at the first Indian village on the headwaters of the Tananá, June 10,
1885. Here Indian cunning, stimulated by curiosity and emboldened
by our starved and helpless condition, surpassed our watchfulness, as
shown by the fact that the hygrometer was stolen, and the barometer
rendered useless by the results of the earnest endeavor of the natives
to understand the nature of its interior construction. From this time
no instrumental observations were taken except those for latitude and
longitude. A daily journal of general meteorological import was,
however, kept throughout the whole expedition, a synopsis of which,
together with tables deduced therefrom, accompanies this report.

So much has been written about the agricultural resources of
Alaska, both *pro* and *con*—of extravagant claims on the one hand,
and of earnest denial on the other—that it is doubly fortunate that
I am able to present the data from which my conclusions are drawn.

I believe that lettuce, radishes, turnips, beans, peas, potatoes, car-
rots, and possibly buckwheat and barley, can be raised in favored
localities on the Middle and Upper Yukon and Tananá in sufficient
quantities to form an important auxiliary to the fish diet of the natives, and to assist in supporting those white men whom business
compels to reside in that portion of the Territory. In the Copper
River Valley conditions similar to those on the Yukon do not exist.
The amount of precipitation and the humidity of the atmosphere,
as evidenced by the tables, show a climate for that region north of
Tarál unlike that of any other portion of the Territory, and in my
opinion the results that could be obtained would not justify an
attempt at agriculture. In the coast regions, sunlight, that element
so imperatively necessary to agricultural growth and development, is
largely wanting. Here dense fog, low *stratus* and *nimbus* clouds
continually intercept their impenetrable masses between the sun's
rays and those unfortunate beings whom nature has placed in these
localities. I use the term "unfortunate beings" advisedly, for certainly it would be hard to find a more miserable and wretched class
of people anywhere than those we found on the coast near the mouth
of Copper River. Nature has furnished them food in the marine
life that fills those waters, but has left them little else to be thankful
for.

The climatic conditions mentioned above are caused by the natural
features of the country. As will be seen by a glance at the maps,
a branch of the Rocky Mountains enters the Territory from the British

possessions about 15 miles from the coast, and takes the name of Alaskan Mountains. They extend WNW. for about 175 miles, at which point they are about 200 miles from the coast. Here they gradually turn to the SW., and after reaching the coast are continued as the Aleutian Islands, and finally disappear in the Pacific Ocean after extending SW. about 600 miles. Another range of mountains, in which is Mount Saint Elias and some other high peaks, extends from where these Alaskan Mountains enter the ocean along the southern coast, and joins them again in the British possessions. The territory inclosed by these two ranges of mountains is about 100 miles north and south, and 200 east and west. It is drained by the Copper River and its tributaries, the former beginning its way through the coast range at Wood's Canon, and emptying into the North Pacific Ocean. These two ranges are so high that they shut out nearly all the moisture from this region, both from the Pacific on the south, and from Bering Sea on the west.

John Bremner, a miner, who passed the winter of 1884–'85 at Tarál, told us that the snowfall during the winter was much less than he had anticipated, and even that was of an exceedingly light and dry character. The conditions we found during our journey verified his statements regarding precipitation. The rains during our travels in that region were very light. The habits of the natives, the fact that this is the only place in the Territory where salmon are cured by sun alone, as far as I know, and the amount of water discharged by the Copper River, all tend to prove that the rain king seldom invades this valley in force. But in the Yukon Valley different climatic conditions exist, owing to different natural features of the coast regions.

From Bristol Bay north for 400 or 500 miles the coast is bathed by the same warm Japan current, and the same humid atmosphere prevails that characterizes the coast climate farther south, as is shown by an inspection of Table IV; but, unlike the southern regions, this moisture is not condensed on the coast. The low coast mountains allow it to be borne up the Yukon Valley and into the interior, where it is precipitated in the form of rain and snow. Hence the 8, 12, and even 15 feet of snowfall in the Yukon Valley, as contrasted with the much less depth in the Copper Valley, as stated by Bremner, is not to be wondered at. The same contrast in the summer precipitations is shown by the records appended.

At Sitka, Nuchek, and Oonalaska, owing to the proximity of high mountain ranges, a large portion of the moisture of the atmosphere is condensed, causing those everlasting clouds, and rains with an annual precipitation of from 103 to 158 inches. But on the western coast these high mountains are replaced by others low enough to allow a large quantity of this moisture to pass over them into the interior, where it is precipitated over the territory drained by the Yukon and its tributaries, and finally finds its way back to the coast again by the mouth of the former—that mighty river which for volume of water discharged is supposed to be second only to the great Mississippi on the American continent.

It is a well-known scientific fact that vegetable life requires for its growth and development heat and moisture, and heat, too, supplied by the sun's rays. Now, in the Copper River Valley one of these elements, moisture, appears to be wanting, while in the coast regions the other, sunlight, is also wanting; hence my reasons for claiming that in neither of these regions can agricultural labors be entered upon with any prospects of remuneration. But in the Yukon Valley both these elements are present in sufficient quantities to appear to justify me in claiming, as I have, that certain kinds of the hardy vegetables may be raised there in certain localities. These claims are also sustained by the results of such agricultural experiments as have been attempted from time to time in this valley. A trader by the name of McQuisten told us that at Nuklúkyet he had grown turnips weighing 6 pounds, also onions and potatoes of good size and quality. The same things have also been produced at Nuláto and Fort Yukon, with the addition at the latter place of barley, which was sown and reached maturity during two successive years, the only ones in which it was tried. The grains were complete and well formed, though the straw was short.

It might at first seem incredible that vegetables of any kind could be raised in these high latitudes, where the frost king of the north is supposed to reign supreme; but when, during the short Arctic summer, the giver of light and heat to this solar system ascends his throne over those northern regions, the frost king retires, and under the sun's life-giving and invigorating rays vegetable life is stimulated to great activity. On the Middle and Upper Yukon the thermometer, when exposed to the direct rays of the sun, has been known to read 112° and 115° Fahr. This, together with the fact that at this season of year the sun is almost continuously above the horizon, will account for the small number of days required for some of the more hardy vegetables to reach maturity. The short summer season of these latitudes is, in consequence, more effective than the same number of days farther to the southward.

The soil is generally of a sandy or clayey loam, mixed in places with vegetable matter and covered with a thick coating of moss. At a depth of 1 to 2 feet below the surface the soil usually remains frozen the year round. This is owing to the non-conductive nature of its moss covering. But the presence of ice at such a depth below the surface would not necessarily interfere with agricultural pursuits; besides, by cultivation and proper drainage, the distance of the ice bed below the surface would be considerably increased.

ABSTRACT OF JOURNAL.

Date. 1885.	State of weather. A. M.	P. M.	Wind.	Remarks.
Mar. 20	Fair	Cloudy	E.	Left Núchek at 10 a. m.
21	Light rain	Heavy rain	E.	Traveled all day.
22	Heavy rain	Light rain	E.	Started at 2.15 a. m.; strong head wind and heavy sea; cold.
23	....do	Heavy rain	E.	Started at 2 a. m.; blowing a gale.
24	....do	....do	E.	Blowing a gale; remained in camp.
25	Cloudy	....do	E.	Started at daylight; reached Copper River.
26	Heavy rain	....do	E.	Wind cold and cutting; some sleet.
27	Light rain	Light rain	E.	Do.
28	....do	Cloudy	E.	Wind lighter and less cold.
29	Fair	....do	SE.	Wind light.
30	Heavy rain	Lt. rain and cloudy.	SE.	
31	Light rain	Lt. rain and sleet...	SE.	Very cold and disagreeable.
Apr. 1	Hy. rain and sleet ..	Hy. rain and sleet ..	SE.	Strong wind; very cold.
2	Lt. rain and sleet...	....do	SE.	Cold.
3	...do	Fair; cloudy........	0	P. m. quite warm.
4	Fair	Fair	0	Traveled nearly all night.
5	Clear	....do	0	
6	Fair	Cloudy	0	
7	Sleet and snow	Sleet and snow	SE.	
8	Light snow	Light snow	SE.	
9	Clear	Fair	....	Reached Tarál.
10	....do	Clear	....	
11	Fair	Fair	SE.	Cold.
12	Clear	....do	0	Warm and pleasant.
13	Light snow; fair ...	....do	E.	
14	Fair	....do	E.	Cold.
15	Clear	Clear	E.	Night cold.
16	....do	....do	0	
17	....do	Fair; cloudy........	E.	Lunar halo, 2 p. m.
18	....do	Clear	0	
19	....do	....do	0	Nicolai's house on Chittystone River.
20	....do	Fair	0	
21	Fair	Cloudy	SE.	
22	....do	Fair	SE.	
23	....do	Clear	SE.	Very little wind.
24	Cloudy	Cloudy	NW.	Cold.
25	....do	....do	NW.	Do.
26	Fair; cloudy........	Lt. rain and snow ..	NE.	Wind light and not very cold.
27	Light snow; fair....	Fair	0	
28	Clear	....do	0	Solar halo, p. m.; aurora during night.
29	Light snow; fair....	Cloudy	....	Light puffs of wind up and down river.
30	Light sleet; fair	Fair	....	Do.
May 1	Fair	....do	SW.	Warm and pleasant.
2	Light rain	Light rain	E.	Wind strong and cold.
3	Fair	....do	NE. SW.	
4	Sleet and snow	Sleet ; fair.........	SW.	Reached Tarál 4 p. m.; saw blue violet in bloom.
5	Clear	Clear	0	Barometer reads 29.50.
6	....do	....do	0	Day warm; night cold.
7	....do	....do	E.	Appearance of mosquitoes; warm; geese and robins.

ABSTRACT OF JOURNAL WITH REDUCTIONS.

Date.	Hour.	Barometer.	Thermometer, exposed.	Thermometer, wet bulb.	Dew point.	Relative humidity.	Wind.	Weather.	Remarks.
1885.									
May 8	6 a. m.....	29.15	44.5	40.5	34.5	68	E.	Fair	cum. st.
8	9 p. m.....	29.05	49	43	34	56	0	...do	4 cum.
9	5 a. m.....	29.10	42	39	34	73	E.	Lt. rain .	Cold rain.
9	8.30 p. m..	29.17	51	45	37	59	E.	Cloudy .	8 cum. and clear.
10	5 a. m.....	29.22	58	52	46	64	E.	Clear ...	
10	10 p. m....	29.18	48	40	26	42	0	...do	3 cum.
11	5 a. m.....	29.20	38	31	17	41	0	...do	Cottonwood buds opening.
11	9 p. m.....	28.80	47	44	40	77	0	Fair	7 cum. st.
12	5 a. m.....	28.78	43	39	33	68	....	Clear ...	Day very hot.
12	10 p. m....	28.62	53	46	37	55	0	Cloudy .	10 cir. cum.
13	6 a. m.....	28.75	45	40	32	60	0	...do	8 cir.
13	9 p. m.....	28.69	48	41	30	50	0	Fair	5 cum.
14	4 a. m.....	28.69	49	44	37	63	E.	Lt. rain .	Rainbow a. m.; strong wind.
14	6 p. m.....	28.60	51.5	46	39	62	E.	Cloudy .	10 cum. st.
15	4 a. m.....	28.63	54	42	20	26	E.	Fair	4 cum.
15	9.30 p. m..	28.63	46	38	23	38	0	Clear ...	
16	4.30 a. m..	28.70	49	40	24	36	0	...do	
16	10 p. m....	28.63	48	38	18	29	0	...do	2 cum.
17	6 a. m.....	28.58	45	38	25	45	E.	Cloudy .	10 cum. st.
17	8 p. m.....	28.15	45	40	32	60	E.	...do	Cold, strong wind.
18	5.15 a. m..	28.13	46	40	30	53	0	...do	10 st.; cold wind.
18	9.15 p. m..	28.05	47.5	40	28	48	E.	...do	8 cum. st.
19	4.30 a. m..	28.15	46	40.5	31	56	E.	Fair	10 st.
19	6 p. m.....	28.15	46	43	39	76	E.	Lt. rain .	5 cum.
20	6 a. m.....	28.23	48	43	36	63	0	Clear ...	10 nim.; clouds high.
20	9.30 p. m..	28.24	45	39	29	53	0	...do	2 cum.
21	5 a. m.....	28.25	42	38	31	65	0	...do	
21	9 p. m.....	28.03	46	35	7	19	0	...do	Ice ½ inch thick in tin cup during night.
22	4 a. m.....	28.03	49	40	24	37	SW.	...do	No p. m. observation.
23	8 p. m.....	27.74	55	44	26	32	SW.	Cloudy .	9 cum.; day fair; thunder, with little rain.
24	5 a. m.....	27.82	46	41	33	61	SW.	Fair	5 cum.
24	10 p. m....	27.65	49.5	44	36	60	SW.	Clear ...	
25	5 a. m.....	27.70	41.5	39	35	75	W.	Cloudy .	Last part of a. m. fair.
25	9.30 p. m..	27.60	46.5	45	40	79	0	...do	10 st.; p. m. showery, with thunder.
26	6 a. m.....	27.60	44	43	39	83	0	...do	Rained some during night.
26	9.30 p. m..	27.65	46	41	33	60	0	...do	10 cum. st.; cold and showery.
27	6 a. m.....	27.65	43	39.5	34	71	0	...do ...	10 cum. st.; rained during night.
27	10 p. m....	27.58	43	39	33	68	0	...do	10 st.; p. m. light rain.
28	5 a. m.....	27.78	43	38.5	31	63	0	Fair	4 cum.
28	9.30 p. m..	27.94	41.5	38	32	70	W.	Cloudy .	10 cum. st.; day fair.
29	5 a. m.....	27.92	41	37	30	65	W.	...do	10 cum. st.
29	10 p. m....	27.90	44	38	27	51	0	Fair	5 cum.; cloudy nearly all day.
30	6 a. m.....	27.91	46	39	27	47	0	...do	4 cir. cum.; night cool.
30	10 p. m....	27.88	46	38	37	35	W.	Cloudy .	Temp. water 43°, 9 cum.
31	5 a. m.....	27.88	53	46	37	55	0	Clear ...	Began to cloud up by noon.
31	....	....	.....	.....	.....	.....	0	Cloudy .	Traveled till late at night.

ABSTRACT OF JOURNAL WITH REDUCTIONS—Continued.

Date.	Hour.	Barometer.	Thermometer, exposed.	Thermometer, wet bulb.	Dew point.	Relative humidity.	Wind.	Weather.	Remarks.
1885.									
June 1	....	......	......	......	......	......	0	Lt. rain.	Light rain all of a. m.
1	10 p. m....	27.40	46	41	33	60	0	Cloudy .	8 cum.
2	6 a. m.....	27.40	44	40	34	68	0	...do	10 cum. st.; p. m. light rain.
3	8 p. m.....	27.10	49	45	40	71	SW.	Lt. rain.	10 nim.; rain very light.
4	6 a. m.....	27.12	49	41	28	44	0	Cloudy .	10 cum. st.; strawberry blossoms.
4	10 p. m....	26.84	41	36	27	57	0	Clear ...	At the foot of Alaskan Mountains.
5	7 a. m.....	26.84	49	41	28	44	0	...do	Began to cloud up early in a. m.
5	10.30 p. m.	26.53	36	27	8	30	0	...do	Fair p. m.; flowers on mountains.
6	5 a. m.....	26.64	41	34	19	40	0	...do	Clear and warm.
6	10 p. m....	26.90	48	39	22	35	0	...do	Do.
7	7 a. m.....	26.90	52	41.5	22	30	0	...do	Hot day; traveled till 11 p. m.
8	9 a. m.....	26.50	50	39	17	27	0	...do	Traveled all night.
9	1 a. m.....	......	......	......	......	......	0	....	Reached summit of Alaskan Mountains.
10	6 p. m.....	......	58	56	54	87	0	Clear ...	Warm, moist atmosphere.

ABSTRACT OF JOURNAL.

Date.	State of weather.			Remarks.
1885.	A. M.	P. M.	Wind.	
June 11	Clear	Fair and cloudy	0	Atmosphere warm and humid; hygrometer stolen.
12	....do	Clear	0	Very warm; vegetation very luxuriant.
13	....do	...do	0	Very warm; natives appear consumptive.
14	....do	Fair	NW.	Wind strong up river during p. m.
15	....do	Clear	NW.	Air smoky; large fires to the west.
16	....do	Fair	NW.	Warm; natives appear consumptive.
17	Cloudy	Light rain	W.	Cooler; flies numerous.
18	Light rain	Cloudy; light rain..	NW.	Rained quite hard at times.
19	Fair	Fair	W.	Continuous daylight.
20	Heavy rain	Light rain	W.	Rain very much heavier than in Copper River Valley.
21	....do	Cloudy	W.	Rain ended about noon.
22	Fair	Fair	W.	Wind generally up river.
23	Clear	Clear	SW.	Day hot; light wind; few cu. clouds.
24	Light rain; fair.....	Fair	SW.	Wind light; rained nearly all night.
25	Clear; fair..........	Clear	0	Day warm; mosquitoes numerous.
26	Clear	...do	0	Arrived at Nuklúkyet.
27	Fair ....,.........	Showery............	W.	Hot; vegetation rank.
28	Clear	Clear	0	Hot; horse-flies and mosquitoes very numerous.

ABSTRACT OF JOURNAL—Continued.

Date.	State of weather.			Remarks.
1885.	A. M.	P. M.	Wind,	
June 29	Clear	Fair; showery......	0	Hot; moose-flies thick.
30	Fair	Fair	W.	Hot; wind light; generally up river.
July 1	....do	Showery.............	W.	Very warm.
2	Clear	Clear	0	Almost no wind.
3	Fair	Fair	0	Few cu. clouds all day.
4	....do	....do	W.	Do.
5	....do	Showery.............	W.	Rainbow p. m.
6	....do	....do	W.	A. m. calm; p. m. wind light.
7	Clear	Fair	E.	Rainbow, 10 p. m.
8	Fair	....do	W.	Strong wind blowing up the river.
9	Cloudy	Cloudy; light rain ..	W.	Cooler; small amount of rain.
10	Fair	Fair	W.	Pleasant; less hot.
11	Cloudy	....do	W .	Cool.
12	Clear	....do	0	Mosquitoes a torture.
13	Fair	....do	0	Very warm.
14	Clear	Clear	0	Hot.
15	....do	....do	W.	Hot; wind light.
16	....do	....do	0	Hot.
17	....do	....do	0	Very hot.
18	Fair	Showery............	W.	Thunder and lightning all of p. m.
19	Cloudy	Cloudy	W.	
20	....do	Light rain	W.	Rain began at noon; continued p. m.
21	Light rain	Fair	W.	
22	Clear	Clear and hazy	W.	
23	Light rain	Light rain	0	No wind all day.
24	....do	....do	W.	Light wind.
25	Cloudy	Showery............	W.	Do.
26	Fair	Fair	W.	
27	....do	....do	W.	Partly cloudy; clouds cu.
28	Fair; hazy..........	Clear	W.	Very warm; sand-flies a great pest.
29	Foggy	Foggy	W.	Wind strong; cold.
30	....do	....do	W.	
31	Fair	Fair	SW.	Cool; sand-flies a torture.
Aug. 1	Cloudy	Light rain	SW.	Wind blowing fresh.
2	....do	Cloudy	SW.	Rained a little during night.
3	....do	....do	SW.	Reached the Kóyukuk River.
4	Clear	Clear	0	Nearly clear all day; warm and pleasant.
5	Cloudy	Cloudy	0	Vegetation becoming less rank.
6	Light rain	Heavy rain	E.	Growing colder.
7	Heavy rain..........	....do	E.	Cold and disagreeable; wind light; Kóyukuk River rose 4 feet in 24 hours.
8	Cloudy	Cloudy	0	Rained some during night.
9	Fair	Fair; cloudy........	SW.	Rather cool; traveling nearly north; turned back at noon.
10	Cloudy	Light rain..........	W.	Cold; wind fresh.
11	Heavy rain	Heavy rain........	W.	*Heavy rain all day.*
12	Fair	Cloudy	0	Cold.
13	Heavy rain........	Cloudy; showery ...	W.	Very cold; wind strong.
14	Fair	Fair	W.	Cold; wind blowing up river strong.
15	Cloudy; fair........	Cloudy	W.	Saw a star for first time this fall.
16	Light rain..........	....do	W.	Wind light.
17	Cloudy	Light rain..........	0	Natives on the river preparing for winter.

ABSTRACT OF JOURNAL—Continued.

Date.	State of weather.			Remarks.
1885.	A. M.	P. M.	Wind.	
Aug. 18	Light rain	Cloudy	W.	Rain light; day warmest we have had for some time.
19	Fair	Fair	0	Quite warm and pleasant.
20	Cloudy	Light rain..........	0	
21	....do	Cloudy	W.	Reached Yukon.
22	Fair	Light rain..........	W.	Started for coast.
23	Heavy rain	Showery............	0	Begin the trail to Únalaklik.
24	Clear	Clear	0	Beautiful day; traveling on tops of mountains.
25	Fair	Cloudy	W.	Light wind; very little rain.
26	....do ....,.	....do	W.	P. m. late few drops of rain.
27	Cloudy	....do	SE.	Reached coast.
28	....do	Light rain..........	SE.	Wind fresh and cold.
29	....do	Cloudy	SE.	Very little rain, but very cold.
30	....do	Fair	S.	Cold; arrived at Fort Saint Michael's.

METEOROLOGICAL SUMMARY.

TABLE I.

During the march.	Dates.		Total days.	Number of days—				Prevailing direction of wind.	Remarks.
	From—	To—		Clear.	Fair.	Cloudy.	Precipitation.		
Núchek to Tarál.............. ...	Mar. 20	Apr. 8	20	0	4	16	17	E. SE.	Rain very heavy.
Tarál to up Chittystone and return.	Apr. 9	May 4	26	11	12	3	7	E. W.	Wind generally up and down river.
Tarál to Alaskan Mountains.......	May 5	June 4	31	12	9	10	8	E.	Rain light.
Crossing Alaskan Mountains.......	June 5	June 9	5	4	1	0	0	0	
Head Tananá River to Yukon River.	June 10	June 26	17	9	4	4	5	W.	Rain heavy.
At Nuklúkyet, on the Yukon River.	June 27	July 27	31	10	12	9	13	W.	Showery, with thunder.
Nuklúkyet to Kóyukuk River......	July 28	Aug. 3	7	1	0	6	3	W. SW.	Dense fog.
On Kóyukuk River to Yukon River.	Aug. 4	Aug. 21	18	0	5	13	6	W.	Rain generally heavy.
Nuláto to Fort Saint. Michael's....	Aug. 12	Aug. 30	9	1	2	6	4	SW. SE.	Crossing Coast Mountains.

TABLE II.—*Condensed summary.*

Núchek to Tarál..................	Mar. 20	Apr. 8	20	0	4	16	17	E. SE.	Coast region; rain heavy.
Tarál to head of Tananá River....	Apr. 9	June 9	62	27	22	13	15	E. W.	Copper R. region; rain very light; atmosphere dry.
Head of Tananá River to Fort Saint Michael's.	June 10	Aug. 30	82	21	23	38	37	W.	Yukon R. region; rains; mostly hazy.

TABLE III.—*Percentage of the number of days on which precipitation fell in the different regions during the expedition.*

Place.	Percentage.
Coast region	85.0
Copper River region	24.2
Yukon River region	45.1

TABLE IV.—*Comparative rainfall and relative humidity, 1884.* *

Place.	Total annual precipitation.	Mean annual humidity.
	Inches.	
Sitka	110.94	74.4
Oonalaska	155.29	80.6
Fort Saint Michael's	15.50	88.4
Copper River Valley †		53.9

* From meteorological records in the office of the Chief Signal Officer, Washington, D. C.

† Mean of observations taken while the Alaskan Exploring Expedition was ascending the valley in 1885.

TABLE V.—*Observations taken at Nuklúkyet.* *

Kind.	Year.	January.	February.	March.	April.	May.	June.	July.	August.	September.	October.	November.	December.
Max. temperature	1882								79	60	52	36	30
Max. temperature	1883	22	37	46	51	72							
Min. temperature	1882								+30	+23	—21	—30	—52
Min. temperature	1883	—43	—43	—37	—10	+42							

* Compiled from records in the office of the Chief Signal Officer, Washington, D. C.

The greatest degree of cold ever known in the Territory was 70° below zero, of Fahrenheit; but such cold is very rare.—DALL.

At Fort Yukon I have seen the thermometer at noon, not in the direct rays of the sun, standing at 112°, and I was informed by the commander of the post that several spirit thermometers, graduated up to 120°, had burst under the scorching sun of the Arctic midsummer.—DALL.

TABLE VI.—*Mean temperatures.* *

Seasons.	Saint Michael's, lat. 63° 28′ N.	Nuláto, lat. 64° 40′ N.	Fort Yukon, lat. 66° 34′ N.
Spring	+24.3	+23.9	+14.2
Summer	53	60	59.7
Autumn	26	+36	+17.4
Winter	+ 8	—14	—23.8

* Compiled from records in the office of the Chief Signal Officer, Washington, D. C.

I am, very respectfully, your obedient servant,

FRED W. FICKETT, B. S.,

Private Signal Corps U. S. A.

Lieut. H. T. ALLEN,

Commanding Alaskan Expedition of 1885:

o